# CRITICAL ACCLAIM

"You will be exhilarated by the opportunities he describes, sobered by his claim that we have it within our power to 'redefine life'."

**Willis Harman, former President of The Institute of Noetic Sciences, author of *Global Mind Change***

"Petersen will enlighten you about the future as probably no one has since John Naisbitt came out with Megatrends in the '80s."

***Milwaukee Business Journal***

"John Petersen correctly puts his finger on the issues that modern civilization and its leadership must confront."

**Edgar Mitchell, SCD, Astronaut**

"Petersen 'maps the edges,' helps change our minds – and thus, the future."

**Harlan Cleveland, President, World Academy of Art & Sciences**

"John Petersen brings remarkable insight to the identification of emerging trends and their implications for the future. He is a true 'out of the box thinker.'"

**Peter Schwartz, founder of the Global Business Network, author of *The Art of The Long View***

"John is unique among futurists because he understands that getting to the future is never a linear event. He has a wonderful ability to encourage our insight, intuition and experience (and not just trend data) to take us forward into both probable and desired futures."

**Margaret J. Wheatley, author of *Leadership and the New Science*, and *A Simpler Way* (co-author)**

"Thank you for giving us a glimpse of the future and some of the exciting things that are going on right now. We are in your debt for stretching our minds and making us think like futurists."

**Mike Steiner, President, The Washington, DC Rotary Club**

"John Petersen's skills and wisdom as a futurist are widely recognized among members of the World Future Society . . . he's a popular speaker among futurists."

**Edward Cornish, President, The World Future Society**

Library of Congress Cataloging in Publication Data
Petersen, John L., 1943-
Out Of the Blue: Wild Cards and Other Big Future Surprises,
How to Anticipate and Respond to Profound Change

Petersen, John L., 1943-
        Out of the Blue: Wild Cards and Other Big Future Surprises
    /John L. Petersen —1st ed.
        p. cm.
        Includes bibliographical references.
        ISBN: 0-9659027-2-2
        1. Social prediction.   2. Forecasting.   3. Business planning.
        4. Disasters — Forecasting.   5. Twenty-first century—Forecasts.
    I. Title
    HN17.5.P48 1997                303.49
                                   QBI97-40754

Please direct requests for reprint permission
and inquiries about Mr. Petersen's presentations to:

The Arlington Institute
John L. Petersen
2101 Crystal Plaza Arcade, Suite 136
Arlington, VA 22202
703.243.7070  •  fax 703.243.7086
johnp@arlinst.org  •  www.arlinst.org

Publisher:  The Arlington Institute
Editors:  Ellen Crockett, Danielle LaPorte, Bayard Stockton
Design:  Paulette Eickman
Author's Photograph:  Diane Petersen
Printer:  McNaughton & Gunn

# OUT OF THE BLUE

## Wild Cards and Other Big Future Surprises

### How to Anticipate and Respond to Profound Change

**John L. Petersen**

A Danielle LaPorte Book

# JOHN L. PETERSEN

John Petersen is considered by many to be one of the best-informed Futurists in the world. Author of the award-winning *The Road To 2015* and a regular commentator for The Voice of America, John's reports on the future have been used at the highest levels of American government as a basis for strategic planning.

He has served in senior positions for a number of presidential political campaigns. He was a naval flight officer, and is a decorated veteran of both the Vietnam and Persian Gulf wars. His DC-based think tank, The Arlington Institute, specializes in helping U.S. Military leaders develop forward-thinking images of a positive future. He envisions a "New Military" that is proactive, preventative, and active in a number of unconventional areas.

When John is not researching and writing, or consulting with the Pentagon, he skis, takes photographs and flies airplanes. He lives in the Washington, DC-area with his wife of thirty years, Diane.

**Futurist:**
**A Futurist seriously and systemically thinks about the future, usually with a professional responsiblity for helping others to identify emerging trends and to explore the implications of change for themselves, their organizations and communities at large.**

# TABLE OF CONTENTS

# TABLE OF CONTENTS

Wild Card Appendix (Continued)

# TABLE OF CONTENTS

Wild Card Appendix (Continued)

# TABLE OF CONTENTS

Wild Card Appendix (Continued)

# ACKNOWLEDGMENTS

You hold this book in your hands primarily because of the very good work of Danielle LaPorte. It was she who pushed the idea, organized the process, managed the logistics and even edited portions of the manuscript. She has also been responsible for all aspects of the book's launching. In a very real way, this is "A Danielle LaPorte Book."

Others have contributed to this volume, most notably Bayard Stockton and Paulette Eickman who responded to short deadlines in editing the manuscript and designing the cover and interior graphics, respectively.

Cindy Wagner, the editor of the the World Future Society's *The Futurist*, reworked some of these ideas for an article in her magazine; in doing so, she kindly made some of the Wild Cards more easily comprehensible. I am grateful to Note Trulock and Mike Farmer for making it possible for me to seriously examine the subject in the first place.

If Ellen Crockett, my executive assistant, had not conscientiously tracked me around the country by phone and email, trying to make sure I was at the right place at the right time, I would certainly have missed deadlines and meetings that were necessary to finish this project. More than that, she built the original Wild Card database when she was living almost a thousand miles away, and our only connection was through cyberspace.

The Arlington Institute is my home base. Its board of directors, Neal Creighton, Jack DuVall, George Kuper, Bob Morse, Dick Sawdey and Jim Woolsey have always (perhaps naively) rallied behind my work. I very much appreciate their support.

And Diane, who has lived with me and loved me for three decades, makes it harder and harder for me to leave town anymore. Still I go, but immediately begin thinking about returning to her again. She makes my hopes for the future bright.

JLP

# PREFACE

I don't know of anyone who has taken a really broad look at Wild Cards before. My friends at the Institute for the Future and the Copenhagen Institute for Future Studies did a very interesting Wild Card study a while ago, but they tended to focus on economic, social and environmental events. The Global Business Network, which kindly allows me to be one of its members, has held a number of meetings on the general subject, but being business-oriented, their unanticipated events have tended to be, well, business-oriented.

Being one who is particularly interested in the leading edge of change, I have often wondered what the full spectrum of big surprise events might be for the U.S., humanity, and the Planet.

From what I see, Wild Cards are an integral component of the equation which combine to generate futures: there are the *driving forces,* and the *crosscutting relationships* that they yield, as well as *Wild Cards*. This book is a simple attempt to deal with big surprises. I trust it provokes you to conclude that thinking about the unthinkable is not only important, but interesting.

I really do believe that we must learn how to deal with uncertainty, with certainty. The number and size of the potential Wild Cards on the horizon make it a necessity.

John L. Petersen
Arlington, Virginia
June 1997

# WILD CARDS

Wild Cards are major surprises. They are high-impact events which come **out of the blue**.

Most of us shrug off an approaching Wild Card . . . if we see it at all . . . because we think we're powerless to do anything about it.

> **Trends:**
> A trend is a general current of change —typically gradual and long-term change—that becomes a directing force for the future.

Wild Cards are not simple trends, nor are they byproducts of anything else. They are events on their own. They are characterized by their scope, and a speed of change that challenges the outermost capabilities of today's human capabilities.

Wild Cards develop very fast. Democratic societies, and the international community of nations, rarely respond effectively because they are unruly and unwieldy institutions. They react to warning with discussion and compromise, rather than with rapid, cohesive response.

But Wild Cards can radically change our outlook, and indeed our lives. Some do so, almost overnight.

# AN EXTRAORDINARY TIME IN HISTORY

We live in a foreshortened span of time, during which we and our environment will change more than during any era in history.

Humanity has never experienced the convergence . . . in some cases, the collision . . . of global forces such as those we may anticipate. Understandably, we have extraordinary difficulty imagining the scope and complexity of the events which are so rapidly coming at us. As the forces merge, recombine, even crash into each other, they cause successive, second- and third-order events — **out of the blue**. When that happens, the whole inter-linked complex catches us, as individuals, communities, corporations, nations, and international bodies, off balance.

**We live in a foreshortened span of time, during which we and our environment will change more than during any era in history.**

Part of the problem is that the developed world's support systems are constantly being reinvented to meet the burgeoning reality of the information age. Yet the very expansion of technological growth means the possibility of information overload and situations where it will be harder to comprehend, much less respond to baffling events.

Dr. Brian Arthur of The Santa Fe Institute, home of the new science of complexity, believes the present information technology revolution is growing more than a million times faster than the historical evolutionary rate of humans and their systems.

**Exponential:**
A geometric progression of numbers (2, 4, 8, 16, 32, 64). Each previous number in a progression is multiplied by a selected number (in this case, 2).

In 1994, the amount of information available in the world was doubling every 18 months. In 1997, it is growing at even faster rates. No field of endeavor has ever grown as rapidly and as globally as today's worldwide information technology industry. In 1996, for example, the number of computers on the World Wide Web grew by 10 percent per month.

We are, in effect, telescoping the time it takes to learn and do things.

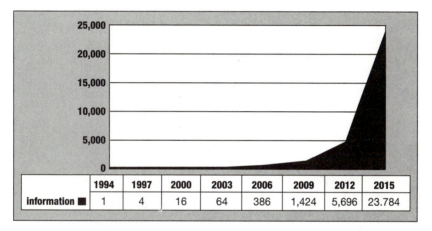

| | 1994 | 1997 | 2000 | 2003 | 2006 | 2009 | 2012 | 2015 |
|---|---|---|---|---|---|---|---|---|
| information ▦ | 1 | 4 | 16 | 64 | 386 | 1,424 | 5,696 | 23.784 |

Amount of information in the world, doubling every 18 months.

If the doubling rate of information only holds constant until 2020 . . . but does not increase as it has been doing . . . **the new millennium will be hugely different**.

This startling rate of change is reflected in other fields which touch our lives. In the coming twenty years the world's population will multiply faster than it ever has before. As long ago as 1989, Ruth Defries and Thomas Malone of the National Research Council warned:

> *During the approximately 4,000 days that remain before the dawn of the third millennium, Planet Earth will be asked to accommodate another billion people – approximately equivalent to the current population of Africa, North America, and Europe combined. Within the next 50 years we must somehow learn to feed, clothe, house, educate, and meaningfully employ an additional 5 billion individuals – the current population of the entire world. Over 90 percent of this increase will take place in developing countries.*
>
> *To accommodate the doubling of the world's population at an acceptable standard of living, a 5-10 fold increase in the productive capacity of the world's agriculture and industry will be required. This is attainable, in principle, through scientific and technological progress, provided humankind makes a long series of small but correct decisions in the management of its affairs. It is theoretically possible for productive capacity to increase 2-fold in 1 decade in developing countries, and in 2 to 3 decades in developed countries.*
>
> Ruth S. Defries, National Research Council; Thomas F. Malone, St. Joseph College: Global Change and Our Common Future, National Research Council, 1989. (emphasis added.)

This means that if you were born in 1950, the Earth's population will likely triple during your lifetime.

Other equally big changes are also taking place in:

- our social values
- science
- technology
- our physical environment

All these forces begin now to converge at an accelerating rate. A collision is imminent. One foreseeable future could well be global instability. Another could be a planetary renaissance. In any case . . . during the next two decades, almost every aspect of life will be fundamentally reshaped.

You may recall The Club of Rome's studies in the 1970s, which dealt with humankind's *problematique*, the complex, cumulative effect on the Planet of certain factors, such as: population, capital, man-

> **During the next two decades, almost every aspect of life will be fundamentally reshaped.**

ufacturing, pollution, land use, and consumption of natural resources. Despite flaws in the methodology of *The Limits To Growth* and *Mankind At The Turning Point*, the problematique the world faces today is ever-more interdependent, ever-more complex, ever-more uncertain. Some of the events envisioned by The Club of Rome's researchers are, indeed, Wild Cards.

In the face of this change, old institutions, methods—even ideas— will collapse. We will have to formulate replacements, quickly. Inevitably, social, economic, scientific and environmental conflicts and revolutions will result from our reactions to **truly monumental occurrences**.

The ensuing chaos will signal a paradigm shift – a divide between one major human era and another – a complete reordering of the way we understand what we today call reality and how things work.

It will be difficult at best to find safe paths through the many hazards confronting us in the unstable ecology ahead. The minefields and booby-traps of great change could cause disaster and, quite possibly, for the first time, our destruction.

# THE CHARACTER OF WILD CARDS

**PUNCTUATED EQUILIBRIUM**   Systems dynamics – the study of the behavior of systems – says that complex systems exhibit a type of behavior called "punctuated equilibrium." It's a term that describes experiences common to everyone. A complex system – a teenager, a company, an economy – does not budge anytime a force is applied to it. It absorbs incoming energy until a critical mass of input builds, and then it moves . . . or changes state . . . quickly, to achieve a new level of stability.

Vice President Al Gore in his book *Earth in Balance* talks about dropping one grain of sand after another to build a slow but stable pile. Suddenly, just one additional, tiny grain causes the cone to collapse – its equilibrium punctuated by change.

**Nanotechnology:** The process of using molecular-sized machines to build useable human-scale products by individually moving billions of atoms or molecules from a raw material feed stock into precise, predetermined configurations.

**CHAIN REACTIONS**     Sometimes the "punctuations" cluster. Because there are so many links between different parts of the human system of systems, one big event could easily begin a chain of events that is much worse than the initial Wild Card itself. The

> Because there are so many links between different parts of the human system of systems, one big event could easily begin a chain of events that is much worse than the initial Wild Card itself.

first one makes the second one more likely, and the snowball starts rolling down the hill. Example: A major natural disaster produces an global epidemic which leads to the collapse of the airline industry.

**SYNERGISTIC EFFECTS**     On occasion, a series of unrelated Wild Cards could come, one after another, with such effect that it shocks the general carrying capacity of the underlying social systems. Here, timing is an issue. If enough body blows come in close proximity for long enough, even if one does not directly influence the others, then the increased amount of chaos associated with fighting fires on many fronts could generate a much greater synergetic effect than the sum of the individual events. The underlying support systems could begin to erode.

> **Nanoplastics:**
> The fusion of plastics with microscopic machines and other objects that are constructed atom by atom. This would result in adaptive, self-organizing products, such as chairs that would remember the preferences of the home's regular inhabitants; and sinks, counter tops, and showers, that would be temperature regulating.

**BOTH POSITIVE AND NEGATIVE** Although it may seem that most Wild Cards are negative, there are many that can also be positive. An energy revolution and the advent of working nanotechnology are two that come to mind that could rapidly change the world for good. Apart from what is already underway in terms of major medical and other research, The Human Genome Project, for example, is itself studded with potentially-dramatic episodes that could quickly spin us off in new directions . . . for instance, discovery of the genetic sequence for intelligence.

Some, like the arrival of extraterrestrial life, could produce either (or both) good and bad outcomes.

> **Human Genome Project:**
> The multi-billion dollar, international project that is underway to map all of the human genetic code, the encyclopedia of all our genetic material that determines the characteristics of most, if not all, organic life on this planet.

**TOO BIG TO LET HAPPEN** The study of Wild Cards is particularly important now because the extraordinarily growing technological capability of humans has produced, starting a few decades ago, **new classes of Wild Cards** which, for the first time have global implications. In some cases scientists believe they could potentially threaten the whole human race. Where before, human activity at worst spoiled a localized piece of real estate,

**One of the things that makes this era unique is the global information system that is rapidly being put in place.**

like Saddam Hussein's torching of the Kuwaiti oil wells, huge strip mines, and the defoliating of the Vietnamese jungles. Now direct and indirect methods are in place of such a scale that the whole planet is threatened.

A large-scale nuclear war is a familiar, but nonetheless-ominous threat. Other Too-Big Wild Cards that are already looming are the possibility of a rapid change in the planet's climate, and the effects of the growing holes in the ozone layer. A potential asteroid-strike would also, of course, be of this scale.

**OUTSIDE FORCES**  One of the things that makes this era unique is the global information system that is rapidly being put in place. Functioning much like a planetary nervous system, as many as seven communication satellite constellations with hundreds of "birds" will be circling the earth soon after the turn of the century, making it possible to send and receive any kind of information from any location on the planet to any other. It will make no difference whether you are in the Sahara Desert or the heart of Wall Street. With a small, inexpensive device you will be in touch.

This information architecture will almost certainly influence, if not cause some Wild Cards. News, rumor and other information will instantaneously sweep across the planet, as accessible to China and Congo as any other place on earth. Similarly, CNN, the Internet, Star TV (and what ever other information delivery systems that are then in place) will act as powerful enablers, carrying big ideas everywhere . . . and thereby making most any significant event more acute.

> **This information architecture will almost certainly influence, if not cause some Wild Cards.**

# THE THREE BIG QUESTIONS

Since by definition Wild Cards tend to be surprises, the usual assumption is that there is nothing we can do about them. Clearly, if we neither take the time to look at them nor consider how they might be anticipated, they are guaranteed to be surprises. Therefore, in a time of high rates of change and uncertainty, the possibility that some major future negative events could be eliminated seems reason alone to look seriously into the new ways of understanding and dealing with Wild Cards.

The process starts by asking three major questions:
- *Which are the most important Wild Cards for me and my organization?*
- *Can we anticipate their arrival?*
- *Is there anything we can do about them?*

We can begin to answer these questions by first understanding the underlying structure – the anatomy – of Wild Cards.

# THE ANATOMY OF A WILD CARD

There are common characteristics which define the big surprises that could shake up the way we live.

A Wild Card :
- Has a direct effect on the human condition.
- Is large, and has broad, important and sometimes fundamental implications.
- Moves so fast that there is not enough warning to allow the rest of the system to adjust to the shock.

Each of these factors must coexist for a potential event to really be significant enough to merit our attention here. If it isn't a big, fast-moving, human-oriented event, it is something else . . . but not a Wild Card.

**THE HUMAN CONDITION**   Wild Cards are significant because they effect an important part of the system that defines humans and how we live.  Although most everything on the planet arguably has some linkage to us and what we do, those that effect us most directly always get our greatest attention. We rate some parts of the human system as more important

> **Wild Cards are significant because they effect an important part of the system that defines humans and how we live.**

than others – or at least a shock to them produces more acute responses. Those are the ones that are most interesting to us.

What we need to do is build a tool that takes into account all the major aspects of the human condition, organizes them in common groups, and then rates them according to the relative importance that each has. That would give us a way to begin to assess how a potential Wild Card might impact us.

**THE TARGET GROUP**   It is hard to generalize about some of these factors. For many people an economic shock would be far more eventful than a big question about the meaning of life. On the other hand, some folks would be convinced that an economic problem would ultimately resolve itself . . . but, if science shows that there really are spirits and ghosts, well, that would change their lives.

So in the end, you, the analyst must decide, relative to your target audience how a particular Wild Card will play. You can cut this in many different ways. If you looked at politicians, they would see the world differently from scientists (or so one would presume.) You might think of your group in psychological terms: inner-directed, outer-directed, and sustenance-driven. Or perhaps you are interested in employees, customers, and regulators. In any case, it is important to know who you are talking about.

For this book we will assume our target audience is the social leadership – opinion leaders.

## THE HUMAN FACTORS

**Being:** There are many things that make up who we are as humans and what we do, but the most fundamental are those things that are associated with being.

- Our understanding of *reality*
- Strongly held personal *values*
- Our health or *wellness*
- The *physical environment* in which we live

**Sustenance:** Our sustenance comes from a number of sources.

- The context or *habitat* in which we live
- The availability and quality of *food*
- The availability of *energy*
- How we *transport* ourselves from one location to another

**Actions:** Then, there are a group of factors that describe what we do, or our actions.

- The way we relate to other individuals — our *personal relations*
- Our *formal group relations* — organizations, governments, etc.
- What we do with most of our time — our *work* and *recreation*

**Tools**: And then, there is that cluster of *tools* or enablers, which we use to make our lives easier and meaningful.

- How we *communicate*
- How we *learn*
- How we make and distribute things
  — our *technology*

If you arrange these hierarchically
they might be represented
as a pyramid, as shown here.

**Tools**

**Actions**

**Sustenance**

**Being**

Terms like economy, government, family, could be substituted for some of the descriptions here, but because we use them so regularly in our everyday life, those words quickly cause us to focus on a common set of assumptions, and therefore make it harder to broadly see potential implications.

The impact of a big event varies dramatically from person to person depending upon how "close to home" it strikes. This, of course, is true geographically, but is particularly true in terms of its effect on one's personal life. If, for example, something strikes at basic beliefs about reality, it would tend to be more powerful than if it dealt with technology or some other area that is more at arm's length from the essence of a person.

We could say that the lower characteristics are intrinsically more powerful in terms of the way they influence behavior. Changes in upper issues, though not at all unimportant, are less profound in the breadth of their influence. Later, we will introduce a process to assess the relative significance of Wild Cards. For

> **The impact of a big event varies dramatically from person to person depending upon how "close to home" it strikes.**

that equation I have assigned relative weights to the four groups of characteristics. The closer they are to defining the essence of who the person is, the larger the score, from one to four. I have called this the **Power Factor** – to represent the relative power a Wild Card appears to have.

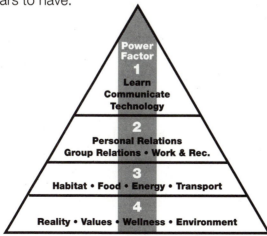

**LARGE, PROFOUND IMPLICATIONS**  Wild Cards are important because they are big – they effect large numbers of people.
Every day we experience personal crises – a death in the family, an
illness, loss of a job, etc. They obviously are important to us, but
they are not Wild Cards, because their influence, although profound,
is relatively local. But when an event causes great change and uncertainty for many people, then it is a candidate for being a Wild
Card.

The "reach" of an event can vary from being a relatively small
number of "important" people (that in turn influence many others)
to everyone on the planet.  It can be a big deal for only one region
of the U.S. (that in time effects the rest of the country,) or could be
a region of the world.  In any case, ultimately large numbers of
people are influenced.

**RAPID STATE CHANGES**   Big trends that evolve over time,
like women coming into the workplace or the anti-war movement
of the 60s and 70s, clearly are important, but they move slowly
enough that the underlying system adjusts and adapts to them.
Not always easily and cleanly – but there is, nevertheless, evolutionary adjustment.

**Wild Cards come fast**. They require a large enough scale of
response that the parts of the system that would usually deal with
them do not have the time and or resources to effectively adjust.

This "surprise factor" can be due to no warning, the fact that an
event was not anticipated and had no apparent early indicators. Or
it can be too big – there perhaps was some warning, but the event
was so large and the inertia of the system was so great that it could
not adapt quickly enough to cope.

Earthquakes, for example, are usually considered no warning
Wild Cards. Hurricanes are ones that are too big. A terrorist attack
is no warning. An energy revolution is too big.

# ASSESSING THE RELATIVE IMPACT

## "Which Are The Most Important Wild Cards?"

Now that we have an understanding of the underlying characteristics of a Wild Card and how they can vary in how they effect us, we can now begin to determine which ones are more important to us and our organization than others.

Because there are so many variables that define a potential momentous event we need a simple process that can be used to quantitatively assess the potential impact of a particular event – compared to others that are out there. This will necessarily be a relative process, biased both by the personal interests of you, the assessor, and by your interpretation of the various factors that make up the basic event. Although the process is relative, it nevertheless will be valuable, for it will be consistently biased across all of the different Wild Cards considered.

We will use the three major characteristics – impact on human systems, large, profound implications, and high rates of change – in a simple relationship that yields relative impact.

### HUMAN SYSTEMS
   • **Power Factor:  The level at which the event effects individuals**

From the earlier discussion of the anatomy of a Wild Card we will use the index which indicates where or how people are effected by the event.

   • **Vulnerability:  How vulnerable is the system or person to the change?**

This relates to complexity and how easy it is for a system to take a hit and come back quickly. It also would include adaptability and readiness.

- **Opposition: Are there those who will oppose this change?**

The degree to which they fight it makes a difference as to how quickly an event effects a person or group. If there are identified groups that will fight hard against the change, it may increase the chaos and lengthen the transition time to the new reality.

- **Timing: Does it happen sooner or later?**

The assumption here is that humanity gains depth, and the ability to deal with shocks the longer we are around. There is more experience, we are more mature. Ten years from now we can handle more things better than we can today. On the other hand, there are events that could get worse the later they happen. The collapse of the Internet is one that comes to mind.

## LARGE PROFOUND IMPLICATIONS

- **Reach: How broad is its effect?**

Is it local, national, regional or global?

- **Outcome: How obvious is the likely outcome?**

It makes a difference in how an event is responded to if there is clarity about what the outcome will be in the end. If the end is uncertain, the response of people will vary and be less effective.

## RATE OF CHANGE

The relative rate of the change. It makes a lot of difference whether an event forces instantaneous change or evolves over a period of time.

Each of these characteristics contributes differently to the impact of a surprise event. I have assigned them the following weighting:

| | |
|---|---|
| **RATE OF CHANGE** (ΔC)<br>faster change = more impact | 1 = years<br>2 = months<br>3 = days |
| **REACH** (R)<br>wider reach = more impact | 1 → 5<br>local → global |
| **VULNERABILITY** (V)<br>less adaptable = more vulnerable | 1 → 3<br>less → more |
| **OUTCOME** (O)<br>more uncertainty = more impact | 1 → 3<br>less → more |
| **TIMING** (T)<br>later events = better outcome | 1 = 2010-2015<br>2 = 2005-2010<br>3 = 2000-2005<br>4 = 1996-2000 |
| **OPPOSITION** (Op)<br>change resistors vs. advocates | 2 → -2<br>much opposition → much support |
| **POWER FACTOR** (P)<br>more individual effect = stronger impact | 1 → 4<br>less → more |

We can combine these factors in the following equation which will produce a weighted index of the relative impact of a particular Wild Card.

The Arlington Impact Index is: Rate of change + Reach + Vulnerability + Outcome + Timing + Opposition + Power Factor

$$\Delta C + R + V + O + T + Op + P = I_{AI}$$

The Arlington Index is an attempt at initial triage. No doubt there will be better ways to assess the impact of Wild Cards in the future, but we believe that this is a relatively inclusive expression.

## QUALITY

The effect of the Wild Card can be positive, negative, or, in some cases might go either way. The quality of individual Wild Cards (see Appendix) gives our estimate of the effect of each.

# ANTICIPATING WILD CARDS

## "Can we anticipate their arrival?"

Most well-known futurists have been surprised. After being confronted by a major unforeseen occasion, a number of futurists, in looking back have found that there were, in every case, indications of the impending event that were not seen as such at the time. If, in fact, there are early warnings that attend big events, then a whole new set of opportunities open up for the strategic planner. For Wild Cards in general, but particularly for those which we really can't afford to allow to happen, early warning would be very valuable.

If there was nothing that we could do, either to anticipate or ameliorate a likely Wild Card, then assessing relative impact would have rather little value. Perhaps those who are responsible for emergency services and disaster relief would find

> **The key seems to be careful, focused and objective observation coupled at times with unusual new methods of accessing information.**

the process helpful, but for most institutions, potential surprises would be interesting at best. It's the same old problem: you couldn't plan for them all and wouldn't know which particular ones to focus on.

But if some of these Wild Cards could be anticipated, then suddenly, we might be able to plan for them and, perhaps in some cases, even keep them from becoming a reality.

The key seems to be careful, focused and objective observation coupled at times with unusual new methods of accessing information. This appears true not only for large, human-engendered events (like those evolving from science and technology) but surprisingly enough, in some cases for natural events which are commonly presumed to be unpredictable. This is basically an intelligence collection — a detective problem. It's a question of finding reliable sources, gathering shreds of information, and making sense out of what comes in.

## FORESIGHT FACTOR

As it turns out, many Wild Cards are surprises to one degree or another only because they were not anticipated . . . and therefore not carefully analyzed. As we become seriously concerned about a particular possibility, day-to-day news items are then seen in terms of that potential event, and if the concern is great enough, then people start to study the issue and look for solutions.

This, by the way, is the reason why scenarios are of such value to strategists. If one has a mental image of a possible future, then news reports and other daily events are assessed with that possibility in mind, expanding greatly their potential meaning.

There are some Wild Cards, especially those having to do with natural events, for which extraordinary means of anticipation are required. Some thoughts on that subject are found in the next section.

So, in terms of the categorization of the Wild Cards in the Appendix, we will assign a foresight factor that reflects our assessment of the theoretical potential of anticipating the event. We know, for instance, that technology is now available that allows the prediction of earthquakes to a high degree of accuracy in terms of time, location and intensity. We would therefore give a high foresight factor to an earthquake-based Wild Card. (As should be obvious from this example, the methods of anticipation may not be well-known or generally understood . . . or these events would not be considered surprises.)

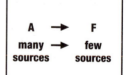

**FORESIGHT FACTOR**
levels of foresight available

A ➔ F
many ➔ few
sources    sources

# DEALING WITH WILD CARDS

## "Is there anything we can do about them?"

Something can be done about Wild Cards. When the best information is available, a new understanding of the potential problem is much more likely to expose the possibility of a new direction of action which will ultimately defuse the Wild Card before it erupts . . . or give one a head start on taking advantage of the big change. There are things which we as societies now handle routinely that perhaps only decades ago would have been big surprises.

We learn from thinking about these events. We figure out how they work and put in place what is needed to ameliorate them. But it is important to understand that most of these answers and indicators will not be found in the usual places . . . or we would know about them.

A systematic, open-minded approach to Wild Cards will revolve around at least three basic rules. The fundamental rule is:

> **RULE I: If you don't think about them *before* they happen, all of the value in thinking about Wild Cards is lost.**

After it happens, it's too late — it's a surprise that wasn't anticipated — and maybe a crisis. If one believes that there will be an increasing number of Wild Cards in the coming years, then the only effective weapon is to begin thinking about them now in a systematic manner.

It should also be noted that the more that is known about a potential event, the less threatening it becomes — the more obvious seem the solutions.

No matter what the a potential Wild Card is,

RULE II:  Accessing and understanding information is key.

Whether it has to do with identifying early warning signs, understanding the structure of a Wild Card or developing a potential response, in all cases the power of the process revolves around a
sophisticated and effective information gathering and analysis process. In this day and age, it requires the input from experts in systems behavior, the Internet, many different traditional disciplines,
and complexity theory and other so-called new sciences.  Access
to a robust network of resource people is a must, and constant
outreach through conferences, conventions and other professional
meetings provide a link to other individuals and ideas that otherwise wouldn't be in one's field of view.

Because we are moving into a new period where potential events
outstrip our existing capabilities for understanding and dealing with
them, it is also true that:

RULE III:  Extraordinary events will require extraordinary approaches.

Some of these potential events look so big, strange and scary because our usual methods of problem solving are not congruent
with events of this magnitude and character. If we are to effectively
deal with them before the fact, a new mind set will be required to
see the potential problems in a different light. For many of them, the
common tools that quickly come to mind (like political, economic
and military influence, to name a few) will not be equal to the task.

We are experiencing a global transition that will result in the
redesign of the fundamentals of human activity.  Those who make

it into the new millennium unscathed will necessarily be the individuals who see unusual new ways to deal with the unprecedented reality that evolves. To be in that group you must unleash yourself from the past and be willing to take the risk of pioneering with new ideas. You must objectively search for **novel tools and perspectives**.

As has been said a number of times, many of the solutions we seek will not come from conventional sources or we would already know about them. Like the equipment that is available that can be used to accurately predict earthquakes, these new answers will come from the fringe. They reside with individuals who look at the world in novel ways and see solutions where others do not. That's where the big breakthroughs have always come from. These people aren't found in the mainstream.

It will require good judgment to identify the potential jewels in places that are inhabited by more than a usual number of misguided individuals and charlatans. But the discoveries are worth the exploration, both for anticipating and planning for surprise events.

## New approaches

Because of the rate of change and scale of their problems, business leaders, among others, are now searching for alternative, nonlinear, methods of dealing with the future. Because of the success of the approach, increasing numbers are attending workshops to learn how to recognize and act on their intuition rather than just using logical methods. There are many examples of

> **It is clear from history that all significant breakthroughs initially appear strange and somewhat unbelievable.**

successful individuals who make all of their major decisions based on "gut feel." A very wealthy oil wildcatter recently told me, "No matter what the geologists and biologists tell me, if I don't feel good about a well, I won't drill it."

This raises an interesting question about how much and what kind of information can be accessed by intuitive techniques. If this tack is seriously pursued, rather quickly one is knee deep in philosophical queries like, "Where does this intuitive information come from?" and "Is the information that I can access limited or is it basically unlimited?" In physics, quantum theory says that everything in the universe is connected to everything else and it is all part of a single information field. If that is so, then perhaps **the answer to any question** is theoretically accessible through intuition or other similar measures.

Even the U.S. government, the former Soviet Union, and commercial organizations have very successfully used extraordinary methods like remote viewing to capture images and impressions from geographic locations and times where human representatives could not otherwise be sent. Accessing a capability that scientists believe is native in all individuals (to one degree or another) scores of intelligence officers have been taught to be able to move their consciousness at will to other geographic locations and both forward and backward in time. The good ones could gather extraordinary visual and audible images and other sensory information of what exists(ed) at the targeted place and time. The U.S. program, whose accuracy was repeatedly confirmed with on-sight inspection, continued for almost two decades. At the present time, commercial consulting firms are available to provide this service for business clients.

**In any case, what we do know for sure is that traditional techniques are not equal to many of the problems we may well have to face in the near future.**

Viewed from a conventional perspective, these notions quickly move one out onto rather unsteady ground. But it is clear from history that all significant breakthroughs initially appear strange and somewhat unbelievable. In this case, there is a proven track record of effectiveness in this general area that suggests that the possibility of a breakthrough in dealing with big, painful events like Wild Cards could be found there.

Some of these unusual techniques may be the only methods that work successfully for some classes of Wild Cards. In fact, they may well be the common approaches that are used for problem solving a decade or two from now.

In any case, what we do know for sure is that traditional techniques are not equal to many of the problems we may well have to face in the near future.

## Different Models, Definitions, and Structures

Since we need new ways to deal with Wild Cards, we should consider most anything that might have promise. We must be willing to develop new models of how things work, different definitions of what is important, and reinvent the big pieces of our social system.

> We must be willing to develop new models of how things work, different definitions of what is important, and reinvent the big pieces of our social system.

New models that should be considered include fractals, organic behavior, systems thinking, intuitive problem solving, and systems dynamics.

The effective response to some Wild Cards will require different definitions of self interest, national security, standard of living, work, cooperation and competition, quality of life, incentives, value, national interest, and rights and responsibilities.

We will almost certainly have to reinvent all or large parts of our educational system, government, methods of doing commerce, families, and military.

It is obvious that this is no small task – it is extraordinary . . . and it is full of risks. But the future holds great opportunities and rewards (as it always has) for those less than faint-hearted individuals and organizations who are willing to actively search for new solutions and plow new ground.

## An Institutional Process

Seriously engaging potential events of the magnitude of Wild Cards requires a comprehensive and sophisticated process. Here is a methodology for identifying, analyzing and tracking these events. It will allow you and your institution to assure that appropriate means are in place to respond in the most effective way to those events which are likely to have the greatest impact. It puts in place a structured system of early warning sensors that pointedly *search* for indicators of important events. It revolves around an effective method of displaying the information from all sources in such a way that trends and relationships — and even the likelihood of actualization — become obvious.

# A Wild Card Process

1. Identify high interest Wild Cards & segment according to options.
   - Those that *must* be addressed.
   - Those that *can or should* be considered.
   - Those events which can only be prepared for (usually revolve around individual natural events – those things for which humans are not the direct cause.)
   - Those events for which there are likely to be no warning.
   - Those events that are potentially too big for the system to adjust to.
   - Those events which may be changed.
   - Those for which a new solution must be invented.
   - Those for which existing tools (education, stockpiling, etc.) can be used.

2. Determine what types of lesser events would point to the coming of a Wild Card.

3. Put in place a dedicated scouting group that is looking for early indicators (traveling, probing, reaching).

4. Assure that *all* organizational units are aware of general concerns and interests.
   - Make the whole system an information gathering device.
   - Have a central clearing house where all of the information is received (probably electronically, perhaps a web site.)

5. Structure incoming information: early indicators, linkages, new events, unknowns, confirmations.

6. Develop an ability to display information spatially in sophisticated ways that quickly suggest what might be happening.
   - Show systems, relationships, early indicators, potential effects.

7. Understand the high interest Wild Cards and decide what can or must be done about them.

8. Put in place a process to influence those selected potential events that can be influenced.

9. Set gates or tripwires that generate increased attention to a particular event as it appears more likely.

## Examples of Wild Cards

In the Appendix which follows, almost eighty examples of Wild Cards will be found. Most, if not all of the major areas where big events might materialize are included, although this clearly is not a complete list of all big surprises that the world might confront. The objective of this collection is to provoke you to consider the variety of Wild Cards that are possible, and to begin to see them in terms that will allow you to see further possibilities.

I have tried to be honest and objective with this list, not eliminating particular ones because of the potential sensitivity of certain individuals or groups. Being less than inclusive for political reasons – particularly with a subject of this importance – would, in my opinion, not be professional, and lack integrity. On the other hand, I do not believe that any of these in particular will happen. I only believe that they are plausible. I have no knowledge about whether any of these are being studied by any group or government. There are no leaks or trial balloons here that I am aware of. On the contrary, my guess is that most Wild Cards are largely being ignored, particularly in the terms that are introduced here.

Wild Cards will not be eliminated. There will always be surprises. But in this time of increasing uncertainty, it would be good to have fewer of them . . . particularly the really big, bad ones. If governments and other major institutions decided that some big events could be anticipated, planned for, mitigated and in some cases, eliminated, then it would be a major new step in human development – a shifting of attention from being exclusively focused on the present and a bit of the past to seriously thinking about the future.

# WILD CARDS

# WORLDWIDE EPIDEMIC

A global epidemic reduces the world population by 50%. Incubating for nine months before symptoms are found, the deadly disease is quickly spread around the world by air travelers. Alternatively, a series of mini-plagues add up to a maxi-plague of diseases such as AIDS, Ebola Virus, tuberculosis, and new strains of influenza. We are "one antibiotic away from disaster" with resistant strains of bacteria.

## POSSIBLE IMPLICATIONS

### REALITY

World population is shell-shocked—we're only interested in staying alive; many societies simply have to start over.

### VALUES

Extraordinary logistical problems would be associated with such a widespread catastrophe.

### WELLNESS

Food and water would be suspect; people might be afraid to go to hospitals, have operations; great fear of getting sick.

### TRANSPORTATION

Collapse of international airline industry as countries quarantine themselves.

### GROUP RELATIONSHIPS

Nations isolate themselves by forbidding travelers to cross their borders in either direction. Much international trade comes to a standstill as disease claims the world's most skilled workers.

# WILD CARD EQUATION

## EARLY INDICATORS

- AIDS and Ebola attacks.
- Resurgence of "old" diseases like tuberculoses.

## FORESIGHT SOURCES

- *The Coming Plague by Laurie Garrett*
- *National Centers for Disease Control*
- *United Nations*

| IMPACT FACTORS | CHANGE SCALE | |
|---|---|---|
| **RATE OF CHANGE** ΔC<br>faster change = more impact | 1 = years<br>2 = months<br>3 = days | **2** |
| **REACH** R<br>wider reach = more impact | 1 → 5<br>local → global | **5** |
| **VULNERABILITY** V<br>less adaptable = more vulnerable | 1 → 3<br>less → more | **3** |
| **OUTCOME** O<br>more uncertainty = more impact | 1 → 3<br>less → more | **3** |
| **TIMING** T<br>later events = better outcome | 1 = 2010-2015<br>2 = 2005-2010<br>3 = 2000-2005<br>4 = 1996-2000 | **4** |
| **OPPOSITION** Op<br>change resistors vs. advocates | 2 → -2<br>much → much<br>opposition support | **-2** |
| **POWER FACTOR** P<br>more individual effect = stronger impact | 1 → 4<br>less → more | **4** |
| **IMPACT INDEX** $I_{AI}$<br>sum of impact factors | 1 → 24<br>low → high | **19** |
| **FORESIGHT FACTOR**<br>levels of foresight available | A → F<br>many → few<br>sources sources | **C** |
| **QUALITY**<br>net effect of Wild Card | + positive<br>- negative<br>± both | **–** |

# HUMAN MUTATION

A mutation occurs in the human race — a dominant mutation — which significantly changes a person's capabilities. New children are born who are quite different from previous generations. Regardless of the source, it becomes rather certain that, ultimately, the basic characteristic/mutation will be passed along to the next generation.

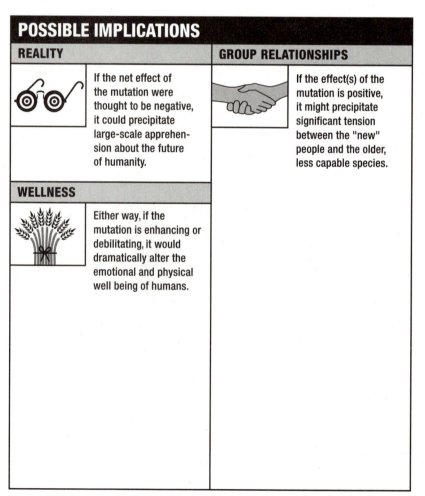

## POSSIBLE IMPLICATIONS

### REALITY

If the net effect of the mutation were thought to be negative, it could precipitate large-scale apprehension about the future of humanity.

### GROUP RELATIONSHIPS

If the effect(s) of the mutation is positive, it might precipitate significant tension between the "new" people and the older, less capable species.

### WELLNESS

Either way, if the mutation is enhancing or debilitating, it would dramatically alter the emotional and physical well being of humans.

- Genetic damage to some children in Russia from large-scale chemical, radiological, or biological pollution (1990).

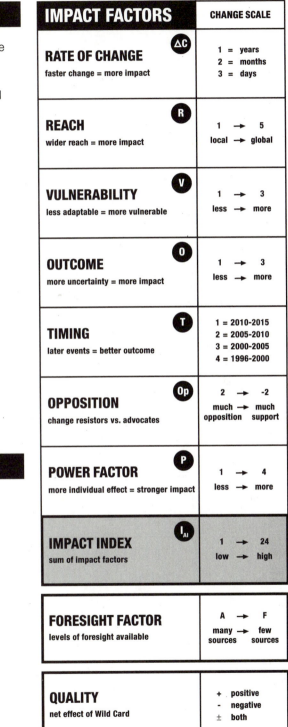

| IMPACT FACTORS | | CHANGE SCALE | |
|---|---|---|---|
| **RATE OF CHANGE** ΔC<br>faster change = more impact | | 1 = years<br>2 = months<br>3 = days | **2** |
| **REACH** R<br>wider reach = more impact | | 1 → 5<br>local → global | **3** |
| **VULNERABILITY** V<br>less adaptable = more vulnerable | | 1 → 3<br>less → more | **3** |
| **OUTCOME** O<br>more uncertainty = more impact | | 1 → 3<br>less → more | **3** |
| **TIMING** T<br>later events = better outcome | | 1 = 2010-2015<br>2 = 2005-2010<br>3 = 2000-2005<br>4 = 1996-2000 | **4** |
| **OPPOSITION** Op<br>change resistors vs. advocates | | 2 → -2<br>much → much<br>opposition support | **-1** |
| **POWER FACTOR** P<br>more individual effect = stronger impact | | 1 → 4<br>less → more | **4** |
| **IMPACT INDEX** I$_{AI}$<br>sum of impact factors | | 1 → 24<br>low → high | **18** |
| **FORESIGHT FACTOR**<br>levels of foresight available | | A → F<br>many → few<br>sources sources | **?** |
| **QUALITY**<br>net effect of Wild Card | | + positive<br>- negative<br>± both | **–** |

- *Dr. Murray Feshbach, Georgetown University*

# HEALTH AND MEDICAL BREAKTHROUGH

A major scientific breakthrough, such as a fundamentally new approach to fighting viruses, proceeds to eliminate many diseases. A wholesale shift occurs in our outlook on many historically deadly diseases.

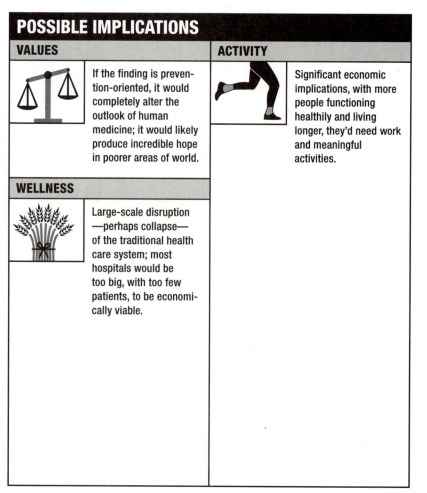

## POSSIBLE IMPLICATIONS

### VALUES

If the finding is prevention-oriented, it would completely alter the outlook of human medicine; it would likely produce incredible hope in poorer areas of world.

### WELLNESS

Large-scale disruption —perhaps collapse— of the traditional health care system; most hospitals would be too big, with too few patients, to be economically viable.

### ACTIVITY

Significant economic implications, with more people functioning healthily and living longer, they'd need work and meaningful activities.

- Great advances in all areas of science.
- Early Human Genome Project findings.

- *National Institute of Health, Human Genome Project*

| IMPACT FACTORS | | CHANGE SCALE | |
|---|---|---|---|
| **RATE OF CHANGE** ΔC<br>faster change = more impact | | 1 = years<br>2 = months<br>3 = days | **1** |
| **REACH** R<br>wider reach = more impact | | 1 → 5<br>local → global | **5** |
| **VULNERABILITY** V<br>less adaptable = more vulnerable | | 1 → 3<br>less → more | **2** |
| **OUTCOME** O<br>more uncertainty = more impact | | 1 → 3<br>less → more | **1** |
| **TIMING** T<br>later events = better outcome | | 1 = 2010-2015<br>2 = 2005-2010<br>3 = 2000-2005<br>4 = 1996-2000 | **2** |
| **OPPOSITION** Op<br>change resistors vs. advocates | | 2 → -2<br>much → much<br>opposition support | **2** |
| **POWER FACTOR** P<br>more individual effect = stronger impact | | 1 → 4<br>less → more | **4** |
| **IMPACT INDEX** I$_{AI}$<br>sum of impact factors | | 1 → 24<br>low → high | **17** |
| **FORESIGHT FACTOR**<br>levels of foresight available | | A → F<br>many → few<br>sources sources | **B** |
| **QUALITY**<br>net effect of Wild Card | | + positive<br>- negative<br>± both | **+** |

# BACTERIA BECOME IMMUNE TO ANTIBIOTICS

Once again, bacteria develop new defenses and become immune to the only antibiotic medicine that now works against them. Staph and other infections explode unabated.

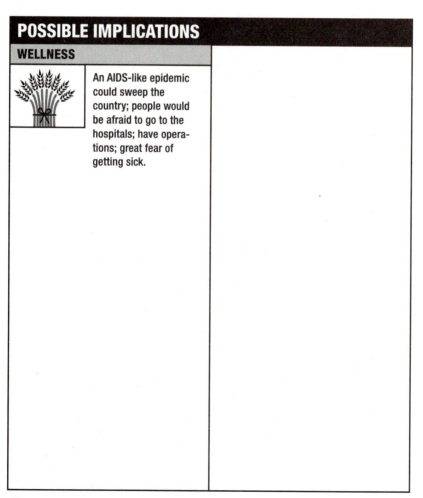

## POSSIBLE IMPLICATIONS

### WELLNESS

An AIDS-like epidemic could sweep the country; people would be afraid to go to the hospitals; have operations; great fear of getting sick.

## EARLY INDICATORS

- In the past, viruses have developed defenses to all but the latest antibiotics.
- Staph not responding to antibiotics in Australia in 1997.

## FORESIGHT SOURCES

- *Center for Disease Control*

| IMPACT FACTORS | CHANGE SCALE | |
|---|---|---|
| **RATE OF CHANGE** $\Delta c$<br>faster change = more impact | 1 = years<br>2 = months<br>3 = days | **2** |
| **REACH** $R$<br>wider reach = more impact | 1 → 5<br>local → global | **5** |
| **VULNERABILITY** $V$<br>less adaptable = more vulnerable | 1 → 3<br>less → more | **3** |
| **OUTCOME** $O$<br>more uncertainty = more impact | 1 → 3<br>less → more | **3** |
| **TIMING** $T$<br>later events = better outcome | 1 = 2010-2015<br>2 = 2005-2010<br>3 = 2000-2005<br>4 = 1996-2000 | **4** |
| **OPPOSITION** $Op$<br>change resistors vs. advocates | 2 → -2<br>much → much<br>opposition support | **-1** |
| **POWER FACTOR** $P$<br>more individual effect = stronger impact | 1 → 4<br>less → more | **4** |
| **IMPACT INDEX** $I_{AI}$<br>sum of impact factors | 1 → 24<br>low → high | **20** |
| **FORESIGHT FACTOR**<br>levels of foresight available | A → F<br>many → few<br>sources sources | **B** |
| **QUALITY**<br>net effect of Wild Card | + positive<br>- negative<br>± both | **-** |

# LONG TERM SIDE EFFECTS OF A MEDICATION IS DISCOVERED

It is determined that a common drug, broadly prescribed for the last thirty years, hastens the onset of a illness such as Alzheimer's, or a similarly debilitating malady. Millions of people are almost certain to contract the disease, for which there is no known cure.

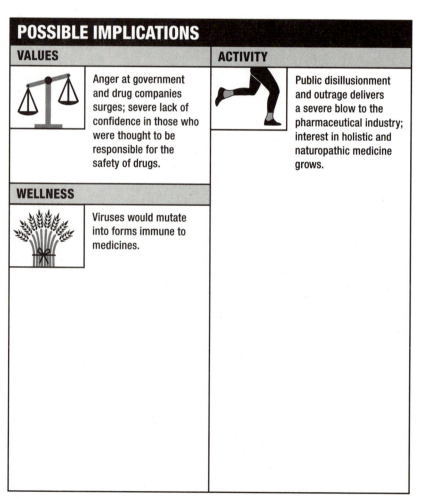

## POSSIBLE IMPLICATIONS

### VALUES

Anger at government and drug companies surges; severe lack of confidence in those who were thought to be responsible for the safety of drugs.

### WELLNESS

Viruses would mutate into forms immune to medicines.

### ACTIVITY

Public disillusionment and outrage delivers a severe blow to the pharmaceutical industry; interest in holistic and naturopathic medicine grows.

- FDA shortening testing for new drugs.

| IMPACT FACTORS | CHANGE SCALE | |
|---|---|---|
| **RATE OF CHANGE** △C<br>faster change = more impact | 1 = years<br>2 = months<br>3 = days | **2** |
| **REACH** R<br>wider reach = more impact | 1 → 5<br>local → global | **3** |
| **VULNERABILITY** V<br>less adaptable = more vulnerable | 1 → 3<br>less → more | **2** |
| **OUTCOME** O<br>more uncertainty = more impact | 1 → 3<br>less → more | **2** |
| **TIMING** T<br>later events = better outcome | 1 = 2010-2015<br>2 = 2005-2010<br>3 = 2000-2005<br>4 = 1996-2000 | **3** |
| **OPPOSITION** Op<br>change resistors vs. advocates | 2 → -2<br>much → much<br>opposition support | **0** |
| **POWER FACTOR** P<br>more individual effect = stronger impact | 1 → 4<br>less → more | **4** |
| **IMPACT INDEX** I$_{AI}$<br>sum of impact factors | 1 → 24<br>low → high | **16** |
| **FORESIGHT FACTOR**<br>levels of foresight available | A → F<br>many → few<br>sources sources | **D** |
| **QUALITY**<br>net effect of Wild Card | + positive<br>- negative<br>± both | **–** |

# BIRTH DEFECTS ARE ELIMINATED

Breakthroughs in prenatal testing and therapy permit doctors to diagnose and treat nearly all birth defects in utero. Gene therapy advances to the point that potential diseases and disorders are eliminated prior to birth. The fully mapped human genome shows doctors where an individual fetus genetic problems are, and advances in nanotechnologies enable microscopic robots to be injected into the body to repair damaged genes.

## POSSIBLE IMPLICATIONS

### VALUES

 Major change in social and economic systems which are all designed for the general life-times and health of present humans.

### WELLNESS

 All children potentially have an equal physical and mental start in life —assuming the therapies are affordable for most families.

### TOOLS

 New industries emerge in nanobioengineering; pharmaceutical companies would invest heavily in the new technologies.

- Advances in aging research.
- Mapping of the human genome.
- Advances in nano-technology research.

| IMPACT FACTORS | CHANGE SCALE | |
|---|---|---|
| **RATE OF CHANGE** $\Delta c$<br>faster change = more impact | 1 = years<br>2 = months<br>3 = days | **1** |
| **REACH** $R$<br>wider reach = more impact | 1 → 5<br>local → global | **3** |
| **VULNERABILITY** $V$<br>less adaptable = more vulnerable | 1 → 3<br>less → more | **1** |
| **OUTCOME** $O$<br>more uncertainty = more impact | 1 → 3<br>less → more | **1** |
| **TIMING** $T$<br>later events = better outcome | 1 = 2010-2015<br>2 = 2005-2010<br>3 = 2000-2005<br>4 = 1996-2000 | **2** |
| **OPPOSITION** $Op$<br>change resistors vs. advocates | 2 → -2<br>much → much<br>opposition support | **2** |
| **POWER FACTOR** $P$<br>more individual effect = stronger impact | 1 → 4<br>less → more | **1** |
| **IMPACT INDEX** $I_{AI}$<br>sum of impact factors | 1 → 24<br>low → high | **11** |
| **FORESIGHT FACTOR**<br>levels of foresight available | A → F<br>many → few<br>sources sources | **c** |
| **QUALITY**<br>net effect of Wild Card | + positive<br>- negative<br>± both | **+** |

- *The Foresight Institute*

# LIFE EXPECTANCY APPROACHES 100

Medical and scientific breakthroughs converge to lengthen the average life by twenty to forty years. Even middle-aged people are quickly grandfathered into the new wave of life extension. Social services, work, and many other assumptions about the past are suddenly up for redesign.

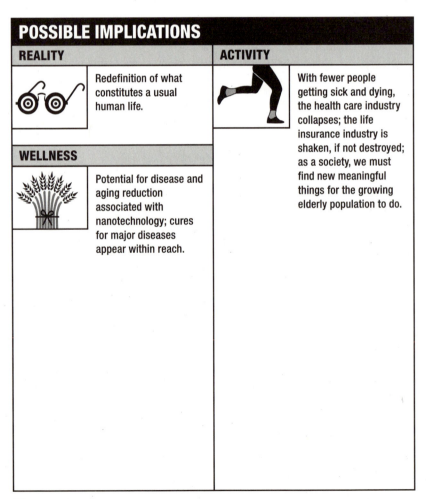

## POSSIBLE IMPLICATIONS

### REALITY

Redefinition of what constitutes a usual human life.

### WELLNESS

Potential for disease and aging reduction associated with nanotechnology; cures for major diseases appear within reach.

### ACTIVITY

With fewer people getting sick and dying, the health care industry collapses; the life insurance industry is shaken, if not destroyed; as a society, we must find new meaningful things for the growing elderly population to do.

- Significant scientific advances being made in cracking the code to aging.
- The growth of "telemedicine," medical guidance through television, is reaching out to typically medically unserved areas.

- *Telemedicine by Maryann Karinch*

| IMPACT FACTORS | CHANGE SCALE | |
|---|---|---|
| **RATE OF CHANGE** $\Delta c$<br>faster change = more impact | 1 = years<br>2 = months<br>3 = days | 1 |
| **REACH** $R$<br>wider reach = more impact | 1 → 5<br>local → global | 3 |
| **VULNERABILITY** $V$<br>less adaptable = more vulnerable | 1 → 3<br>less → more | 1 |
| **OUTCOME** $O$<br>more uncertainty = more impact | 1 → 3<br>less → more | 2 |
| **TIMING** $T$<br>later events = better outcome | 1 = 2010-2015<br>2 = 2005-2010<br>3 = 2000-2005<br>4 = 1996-2000 | 2 |
| **OPPOSITION** $Op$<br>change resistors vs. advocates | 2 → -2<br>much → much<br>opposition support | -1 |
| **POWER FACTOR** $P$<br>more individual effect = stronger impact | 1 → 4<br>less → more | 4 |
| **IMPACT INDEX** $I_{AI}$<br>sum of impact factors | 1 → 24<br>low → high | 12 |
| **FORESIGHT FACTOR**<br>levels of foresight available | A → F<br>many → few<br>sources sources | A |
| **QUALITY**<br>net effect of Wild Card | + positive<br>- negative<br>± both | ± |

# THE ARRIVAL OF ETS — UNAMBIGUOUS CONTACT WITH EXTRATERRESTRIAL LIFE IS MADE

Scenarios: a) Friendly ETs come in peace, bearing technology beyond our wildest dreams — they want to share. b) Unfriendly ETs come to conquer with weapons and technology far superior to ours. c) Some of each — benevolent and menacing species — show up. In any case it is likely that some groups of people who would perceive such an event as a grave threat, and other groups who would see it in terms of opportunity and hope. It would be the biggest thing to happen on earth in recorded human history.

## POSSIBLE IMPLICATIONS

### REALITY

Such a visitation would be fraught with large-scale tension and anxiety. For the majority of people, it would precipitate a fundamental reassessment of the very basics of reality and the role of humans in the universe.

### VALUES

Some religious groups would be greatly threatened, philosophies and long held beliefs would be uprooted and redefined.

### ACTIVITY

Financial markets could be significantly disrupted, driven by the uncertainty of the moment.

- The increasing level of public fascination in this area, as evidenced by blockbuster movies, popular television programs and ET/sci-fi interest groups and paraphernalia.

- Mainline physicists now say that quantum mechanics shows that distance may not present a time problem in traveling throughout the universe.

- Thousands of recent video tapings of UFOs in Mexico have some Mexican authorities convinced that something very unusual is in progress; big UFO flaps in Brazil, Belgium and other countries lend credibility to the possibility.

### FORESIGHT SOURCES

- *National Institute for Discovery Science*
- *Institute of Noetic Sciences*
- *Society for Scientific Exploration*
- *Internet newsgroups*

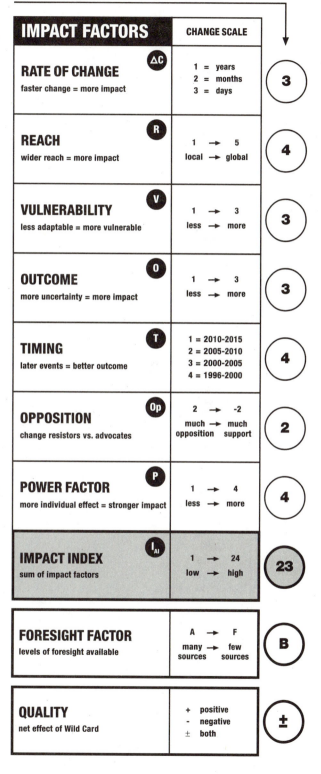

**IMPACT FACTORS** — CHANGE SCALE

**RATE OF CHANGE** ($\Delta c$)
faster change = more impact
1 = years
2 = months
3 = days
→ 3

**REACH** (R)
wider reach = more impact
1 → 5
local → global
→ 4

**VULNERABILITY** (V)
less adaptable = more vulnerable
1 → 3
less → more
→ 3

**OUTCOME** (O)
more uncertainty = more impact
1 → 3
less → more
→ 3

**TIMING** (T)
later events = better outcome
1 = 2010-2015
2 = 2005-2010
3 = 2000-2005
4 = 1996-2000
→ 4

**OPPOSITION** (Op)
change resistors vs. advocates
2 → -2
much opposition → much support
→ 2

**POWER FACTOR** (P)
more individual effect = stronger impact
1 → 4
less → more
→ 4

**IMPACT INDEX** ($I_{AI}$)
sum of impact factors
1 → 24
low → high
→ 23

**FORESIGHT FACTOR**
levels of foresight available
A → F
many sources → few sources
→ B

**QUALITY**
net effect of Wild Card
+ positive
- negative
± both
→ ±

# THE RETURN OF THE "MESSIAH"

An individual who claims to be the "an ascended master" produces extraordinary "miracles" that are witnessed by masses of people. A large percentage of the world's population is convinced that he is, indeed, the Christ returned.

## POSSIBLE IMPLICATIONS

### VALUES

Such an occurrence would call for new global values and objectives; some religions would have a very negative reaction.

### GROUP RELATIONSHIPS

Governments would have to undergo a fundamental reassessment of their relationship to the new leader.

### COMMUNICATION

Television networks would spread word and visual evidence to most of world almost immediately.

- A self proclaimed avatar in India, Sri Satya Sai Baba, is reported to regularly do "miracles." He says that his principal work on earth will begin in 1997 and last for two decades.

- The prophecies and ideals of many major world religions are based upon such an event.

### FORESIGHT SOURCES

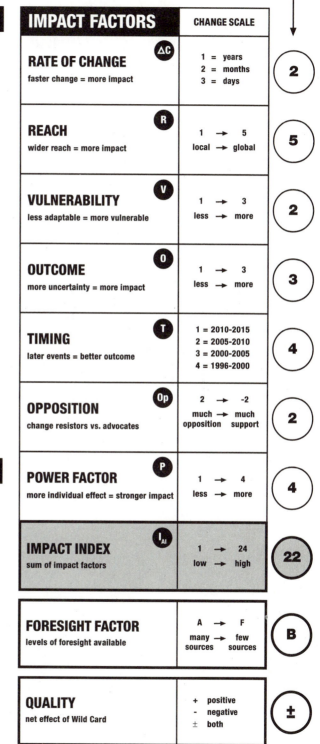

| IMPACT FACTORS | CHANGE SCALE | |
|---|---|---|
| **RATE OF CHANGE** (ΔC)<br>faster change = more impact | 1 = years<br>2 = months<br>3 = days | **2** |
| **REACH** (R)<br>wider reach = more impact | 1 → 5<br>local → global | **5** |
| **VULNERABILITY** (V)<br>less adaptable = more vulnerable | 1 → 3<br>less → more | **2** |
| **OUTCOME** (O)<br>more uncertainty = more impact | 1 → 3<br>less → more | **3** |
| **TIMING** (T)<br>later events = better outcome | 1 = 2010-2015<br>2 = 2005-2010<br>3 = 2000-2005<br>4 = 1996-2000 | **4** |
| **OPPOSITION** (Op)<br>change resistors vs. advocates | 2 → -2<br>much → much<br>opposition support | **2** |
| **POWER FACTOR** (P)<br>more individual effect = stronger impact | 1 → 4<br>less → more | **4** |
| **IMPACT INDEX** (I_AI)<br>sum of impact factors | 1 → 24<br>low → high | **22** |
| **FORESIGHT FACTOR**<br>levels of foresight available | A → F<br>many → few<br>sources sources | **B** |
| **QUALITY**<br>net effect of Wild Card | + positive<br>- negative<br>± both | **±** |

# LIFE IN OTHER DIMENSIONS IS DISCOVERED

Scientific experiments prove the existence of more than three dimensions. Further work verifies that conscious entities – spirits, ghosts, angels, etc. – exist in the spaces which coexist with third dimensional physical reality.

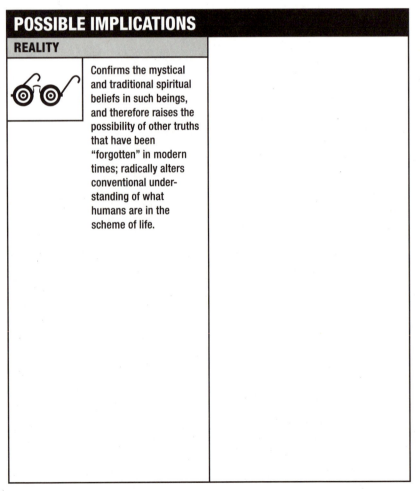

## POSSIBLE IMPLICATIONS

### REALITY

Confirms the mystical and traditional spiritual beliefs in such beings, and therefore raises the possibility of other truths that have been "forgotten" in modern times; radically alters conventional under-standing of what humans are in the scheme of life.

- Quantum mechanics suggests that there are at least ten dimensions to reality (1994).

- Increasingly sophisticated research is being conducted to attempt to isolate other conscious entities, if they exist.

- *Society for Scientific Exploration*

- *National Institute for Discovery Science*

- *University of Virginia*

- *University of Nevada at Las Vegas*

- *PEAR Laboratory, Department of Engineering*

- *Princeton University*

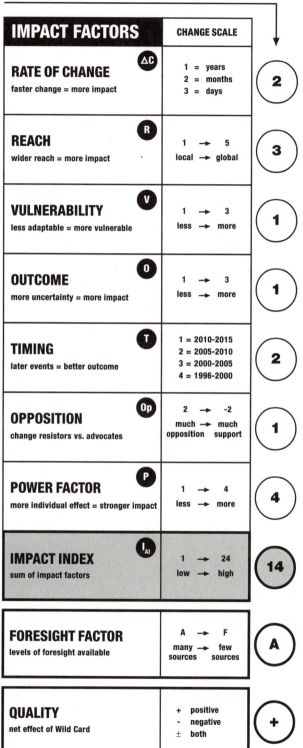

| IMPACT FACTORS | CHANGE SCALE | |
|---|---|---|
| **RATE OF CHANGE** ΔC<br>faster change = more impact | 1 = years<br>2 = months<br>3 = days | **2** |
| **REACH** R<br>wider reach = more impact | 1 → 5<br>local → global | **3** |
| **VULNERABILITY** V<br>less adaptable = more vulnerable | 1 → 3<br>less → more | **1** |
| **OUTCOME** O<br>more uncertainty = more impact | 1 → 3<br>less → more | **1** |
| **TIMING** T<br>later events = better outcome | 1 = 2010-2015<br>2 = 2005-2010<br>3 = 2000-2005<br>4 = 1996-2000 | **2** |
| **OPPOSITION** Op<br>change resistors vs. advocates | 2 → -2<br>much → much<br>opposition support | **1** |
| **POWER FACTOR** P<br>more individual effect = stronger impact | 1 → 4<br>less → more | **4** |
| **IMPACT INDEX** I_AI<br>sum of impact factors | 1 → 24<br>low → high | **14** |
| **FORESIGHT FACTOR**<br>levels of foresight available | A → F<br>many → few<br>sources sources | **A** |
| **QUALITY**<br>net effect of Wild Card | + positive<br>- negative<br>± both | **+** |

# HUMAN GENETIC ENGINEERING ARRIVES: HUMAN CLONING IS PERFECTED

Science develops the ability to produce copies of individual humans. "Duplicate" and "designer" people have predetermined or special physical or mental skills. Significant potential for misuse . . .

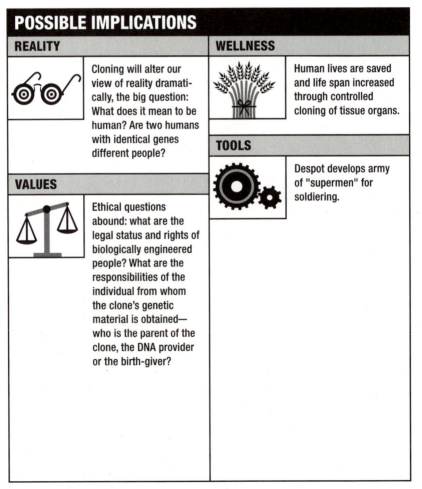

## POSSIBLE IMPLICATIONS

### REALITY

Cloning will alter our view of reality dramatically, the big question: What does it mean to be human? Are two humans with identical genes different people?

### VALUES

Ethical questions abound: what are the legal status and rights of biologically engineered people? What are the responsibilities of the individual from whom the clone's genetic material is obtained—who is the parent of the clone, the DNA provider or the birth-giver?

### WELLNESS

Human lives are saved and life span increased through controlled cloning of tissue organs.

### TOOLS

Despot develops army of "supermen" for soldiering.

## EARLY INDICATORS

- Cloning of cattle (1994).
- Mouse genetically designed with human ear on top of head (1996).
- A sheep cloned by Scottish scientists was born (1996).

## FORESIGHT SOURCES

- *Genetic engineering research*
- *Human Genome Project*

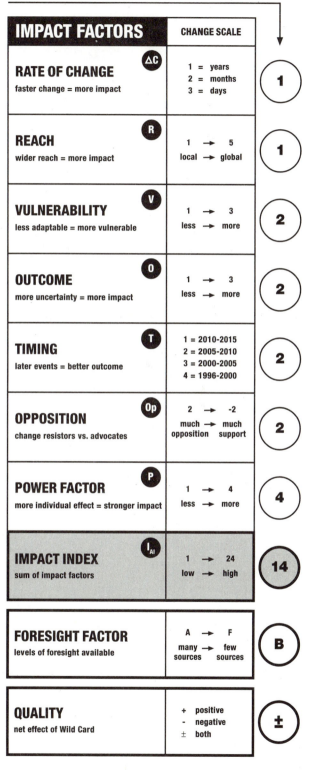

| IMPACT FACTORS | CHANGE SCALE | |
|---|---|---|
| **RATE OF CHANGE** (ΔC) faster change = more impact | 1 = years<br>2 = months<br>3 = days | **1** |
| **REACH** (R) wider reach = more impact | 1 → 5<br>local → global | **1** |
| **VULNERABILITY** (V) less adaptable = more vulnerable | 1 → 3<br>less → more | **2** |
| **OUTCOME** (O) more uncertainty = more impact | 1 → 3<br>less → more | **2** |
| **TIMING** (T) later events = better outcome | 1 = 2010-2015<br>2 = 2005-2010<br>3 = 2000-2005<br>4 = 1996-2000 | **2** |
| **OPPOSITION** (Op) change resistors vs. advocates | 2 → -2<br>much → much<br>opposition support | **2** |
| **POWER FACTOR** (P) more individual effect = stronger impact | 1 → 4<br>less → more | **4** |
| **IMPACT INDEX** (I_AI) sum of impact factors | 1 → 24<br>low → high | **14** |
| **FORESIGHT FACTOR** levels of foresight available | A → F<br>many → few<br>sources sources | **B** |
| **QUALITY** net effect of Wild Card | + positive<br>- negative<br>± both | **±** |

# FUTURE PREDICTION BECOMES STANDARD BUSINESS

Using newly developed techniques and capabilities, it becomes possible to make highly accurate short-range (2-3 month) predictions, including scenarios of what would happen if no one acted on the knowledge of the prediction. It becomes common practice to alert appropriate people of major negative events that are likely if no change is made in the present trends.

## POSSIBLE IMPLICATIONS

### REALITY

Perhaps associated with new understanding of physical reality.

### ACTIVITY

Prevention becomes big business; significant alterations in the insurance industry.

### GROUP RELATIONSHIPS

Futurism becomes a new science made broadly available, possibly as one of the services provided by the government, (much like weather forecasting.)

# WILD CARD EQUATION

EARLY INDICATORS

- Positive track record by government psychic operatives.
- Growing demand for consulting Futurists.
- Other unusual techniques that seem to suggest that the future is accessible.

| IMPACT FACTORS | | CHANGE SCALE | |
|---|---|---|---|
| **RATE OF CHANGE** ΔC<br>faster change = more impact | | 1 = years<br>2 = months<br>3 = days | **1** |
| **REACH** R<br>wider reach = more impact | | 1 → 5<br>local → global | **4** |
| **VULNERABILITY** V<br>less adaptable = more vulnerable | | 1 → 3<br>less → more | **1** |
| **OUTCOME** O<br>more uncertainty = more impact | | 1 → 3<br>less → more | **2** |
| **TIMING** T<br>later events = better outcome | | 1 = 2010-2015<br>2 = 2005-2010<br>3 = 2000-2005<br>4 = 1996-2000 | **2** |
| **OPPOSITION** Op<br>change resistors vs. advocates | | 2 → -2<br>much → much<br>opposition support | **-1** |
| **POWER FACTOR** P<br>more individual effect = stronger impact | | 1 → 4<br>less → more | **4** |
| **IMPACT INDEX** I$_{AI}$<br>sum of impact factors | | 1 → 24<br>low → high | **14** |
| **FORESIGHT FACTOR**<br>levels of foresight available | | A → F<br>many → few<br>sources sources | **B** |
| **QUALITY**<br>net effect of Wild Card | | + positive<br>- negative<br>± both | **+** |

**FORESIGHT SOURCES**

- *Future Memory by Atwater*

# TIME TRAVEL INVENTED

A fantastic breakthrough in quantum mechanics allows us to "engineer" and manipulate space and time – it becomes possible to physically travel both forward and backward in time.

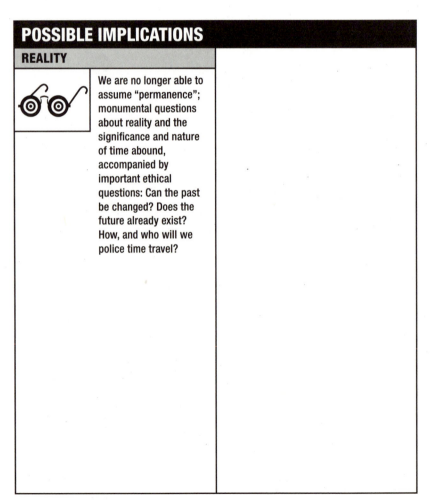

## POSSIBLE IMPLICATIONS

### REALITY

We are no longer able to assume "permanence"; monumental questions about reality and the significance and nature of time abound, accompanied by important ethical questions: Can the past be changed? Does the future already exist? How, and who will we police time travel?

## EARLY INDICATORS

- Proven ability of remote viewers to "see" the future and view the past.

- U.S. Air Force working on faster-than-light travel experiments.

- New understandings of quantum physics are growing exponentially.

## FORESIGHT SOURCES

| IMPACT FACTORS | CHANGE SCALE | |
|---|---|---|
| **RATE OF CHANGE** $\Delta c$<br>faster change = more impact | 1 = years<br>2 = months<br>3 = days | **2** |
| **REACH** $R$<br>wider reach = more impact | 1 → 5<br>local → global | **4** |
| **VULNERABILITY** $V$<br>less adaptable = more vulnerable | 1 → 3<br>less → more | **3** |
| **OUTCOME** $O$<br>more uncertainty = more impact | 1 → 3<br>less → more | **3** |
| **TIMING** $T$<br>later events = better outcome | 1 = 2010-2015<br>2 = 2005-2010<br>3 = 2000-2005<br>4 = 1996-2000 | **2** |
| **OPPOSITION** $Op$<br>change resistors vs. advocates | 2 → -2<br>much → much<br>opposition support | **2** |
| **POWER FACTOR** $P$<br>more individual effect = stronger impact | 1 → 4<br>less → more | **4** |
| **IMPACT INDEX** $I_{AI}$<br>sum of impact factors | 1 → 24<br>low → high | **20** |
| **FORESIGHT FACTOR**<br>levels of foresight available | A → F<br>many → few<br>sources sources | **B** |
| **QUALITY**<br>net effect of Wild Card | + positive<br>- negative<br>± both | **±** |

# ALTRUISM OUTBREAK

Society experiences a passionate good-will movement, strongest among baby boomers. Altruism blossoms everywhere in response to pressing problems, as people decide that they must solve social problems themselves rather than relying exclusively on the government.

## POSSIBLE IMPLICATIONS

### VALUES

Decrease in crimes.

### LEARNING

Institutions such as schools could be revitalized and become more efficient, thanks to community support.

### HABITAT

Inner cities get cleaned up.

### GROUP RELATIONSHIPS

Governments might decrease as more people take care of themselves and each other.

## EARLY INDICATORS

- Recent "random acts of kindness" movement.
- Clinton-Bush volunteerism proposal.
- Large-scale failure of urban school districts.
- Great increase in social problems. Increasing pressures on governments.
- Increasing disparity within society between haves and have-nots setting up situation ripe for future conflict.

## FORESIGHT SOURCES

| IMPACT FACTORS | CHANGE SCALE | |
|---|---|---|
| **RATE OF CHANGE** $\Delta c$ <br> faster change = more impact | 1 = years <br> 2 = months <br> 3 = days | **2** |
| **REACH** R <br> wider reach = more impact | 1 → 5 <br> local → global | **5** |
| **VULNERABILITY** V <br> less adaptable = more vulnerable | 1 → 3 <br> less → more | **3** |
| **OUTCOME** O <br> more uncertainty = more impact | 1 → 3 <br> less → more | **3** |
| **TIMING** T <br> later events = better outcome | 1 = 2010-2015 <br> 2 = 2005-2010 <br> 3 = 2000-2005 <br> 4 = 1996-2000 | **3** |
| **OPPOSITION** Op <br> change resistors vs. advocates | 2 → -2 <br> much → much <br> opposition support | **-1** |
| **POWER FACTOR** P <br> more individual effect = stronger impact | 1 → 4 <br> less → more | **4** |
| **IMPACT INDEX** $I_{AI}$ <br> sum of impact factors | 1 → 24 <br> low → high | **19** |
| **FORESIGHT FACTOR** <br> levels of foresight available | A → F <br> many → few <br> sources sources | **B** |
| **QUALITY** <br> net effect of Wild Card | + positive <br> - negative <br> ± both | **+** |

# FETAL SEX SELECTION BECOMES THE NORM

Do you want a boy, or a girl? A new medical breakthrough provides an easy, safe and inexpensive method to select the sex of the fetus in a planned pregnancy.

## POSSIBLE IMPLICATIONS

### VALUES

Huge skewing of social and economic systems; change in basic notion of families and function of procreation; there is an immediate change in the ratio of births, with males accounting for between 75-85% of all births, in third world countries, the ratio is even higher.

### GROUP RELATIONSHIPS

Fundamentalist religious groups condemn fetal sex selection, moral debates ignite; as the minority gender population, women's rights are trampled —they unite for a revolution; alternatively, women are cherished for their social position and given special privileges.

- Chinese and others are reportedly now aborting females at much greater rates than males.

- *Human Genome Project*
- *Fertility research*

| IMPACT FACTORS | CHANGE SCALE | |
|---|---|---|
| **RATE OF CHANGE** ΔC<br>faster change = more impact | 1 = years<br>2 = months<br>3 = days | **1** |
| **REACH** R<br>wider reach = more impact | 1 → 5<br>local → global | **5** |
| **VULNERABILITY** V<br>less adaptable = more vulnerable | 1 → 3<br>less → more | **3** |
| **OUTCOME** O<br>more uncertainty = more impact | 1 → 3<br>less → more | **2** |
| **TIMING** T<br>later events = better outcome | 1 = 2010-2015<br>2 = 2005-2010<br>3 = 2000-2005<br>4 = 1996-2000 | **1** |
| **OPPOSITION** Op<br>change resistors vs. advocates | 2 → -2<br>much → much<br>opposition support | **2** |
| **POWER FACTOR** P<br>more individual effect = stronger impact | 1 → 4<br>less → more | **4** |
| **IMPACT INDEX** I$_{AI}$<br>sum of impact factors | 1 → 24<br>low → high | **18** |
| **FORESIGHT FACTOR**<br>levels of foresight available | A → F<br>many → few<br>sources sources | **A** |
| **QUALITY**<br>net effect of Wild Card | + positive<br>- negative<br>± both | **–** |

# REMOTE VIEWING BECOMES WIDESPREAD — THERE ARE NO CERTAIN SECRETS

Remote viewing, the ability to mentally/psychically "see" distant locations and future scenarios, becomes popular in civilian circles. Over 2000 individuals become adept and remote viewers hire out their services to commercial clients.

## POSSIBLE IMPLICATIONS

### REALITY

Remote viewing would stir questions of the nature of reality and time.

### TOOLS

The ability to anticipate potential events allows more effective government and institutional policies.

### GROUP RELATIONSHIPS

Military, governmental, and trade secrets become vulnerable; public officials would be challenged regularly on their veracity by those with specific, contradictory information retrieved via remote viewing.

- Very successful two-decade-long CIA-funded project clearly establishes the effectiveness of remote viewing.

- A commercial remote viewing consulting firm is now open for business.

- An increasing number of new books and materials on the subject.

## FORESIGHT SOURCES

- *Society for Scientific Exploration*

| IMPACT FACTORS | CHANGE SCALE | |
|---|---|---|
| **RATE OF CHANGE** $\Delta c$ <br> faster change = more impact | 1 = years <br> 2 = months <br> 3 = days | 1 |
| **REACH** R <br> wider reach = more impact | 1 → 5 <br> local → global | 4 |
| **VULNERABILITY** V <br> less adaptable = more vulnerable | 1 → 3 <br> less → more | 1 |
| **OUTCOME** O <br> more uncertainty = more impact | 1 → 3 <br> less → more | 3 |
| **TIMING** T <br> later events = better outcome | 1 = 2010-2015 <br> 2 = 2005-2010 <br> 3 = 2000-2005 <br> 4 = 1996-2000 | 3 |
| **OPPOSITION** Op <br> change resistors vs. advocates | 2 → -2 <br> much → much <br> opposition support | 2 |
| **POWER FACTOR** P <br> more individual effect = stronger impact | 1 → 4 <br> less → more | 4 |
| **IMPACT INDEX** $I_{AI}$ <br> sum of impact factors | 1 → 24 <br> low → high | 18 |
| **FORESIGHT FACTOR** <br> levels of foresight available | A → F <br> many → few <br> sources sources | A |
| **QUALITY** <br> net effect of Wild Card | + positive <br> - negative <br> ± both | – |

# U.S. ECONOMY FAILS

An escalating federal debt, combined with a high inflation rate and a rash of natural disasters, causes a U.S. financial collapse. Once the downward spiral begins, it is difficult to check.

## POSSIBLE IMPLICATIONS

### GROUP RELATIONSHIPS

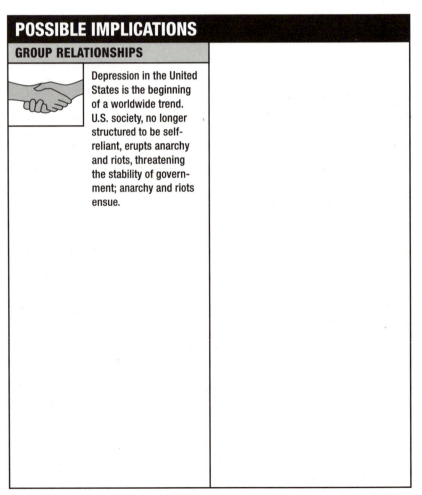

Depression in the United States is the beginning of a worldwide trend. U.S. society, no longer structured to be self-reliant, erupts anarchy and riots, threatening the stability of government; anarchy and riots ensue.

- Federal debt is rising, health care costs are climbing, and more cities and counties are declaring bankruptcy and requesting disaster relief.

- *Wall Street Journal*

| IMPACT FACTORS | CHANGE SCALE | |
|---|---|---|
| **RATE OF CHANGE** $\Delta c$<br>faster change = more impact | 1 = years<br>2 = months<br>3 = days | **2** |
| **REACH** R<br>wider reach = more impact | 1 → 5<br>local → global | **5** |
| **VULNERABILITY** V<br>less adaptable = more vulnerable | 1 → 3<br>less → more | **3** |
| **OUTCOME** O<br>more uncertainty = more impact | 1 → 3<br>less → more | **3** |
| **TIMING** T<br>later events = better outcome | 1 = 2010-2015<br>2 = 2005-2010<br>3 = 2000-2005<br>4 = 1996-2000 | **3** |
| **OPPOSITION** Op<br>change resistors vs. advocates | 2 → -2<br>much → much<br>opposition support | **2** |
| **POWER FACTOR** P<br>more individual effect = stronger impact | 1 → 4<br>less → more | **3** |
| **IMPACT INDEX** I$_{AI}$<br>sum of impact factors | 1 → 24<br>low → high | **21** |
| **FORESIGHT FACTOR**<br>levels of foresight available | A → F<br>many → few<br>sources sources | **B** |
| **QUALITY**<br>net effect of Wild Card | + positive<br>- negative<br>± both | **–** |

# NUCLEAR TERRORISTS ATTACK THE UNITED STATES

A group unhappy with some U.S. policy smuggles an explosive nuclear device into a major port aboard a container ship, (or into an office building via a commercial package-delivery service.) The device is detonated by remote control. A major portion of a city is destroyed, and the fallout closes down the area for a number of years.

## POSSIBLE IMPLICATIONS

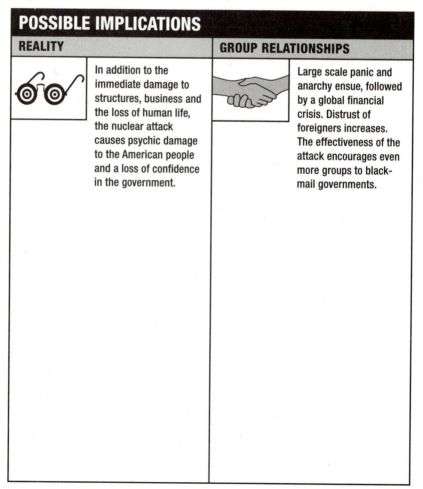

| REALITY | GROUP RELATIONSHIPS |
|---|---|
| In addition to the immediate damage to structures, business and the loss of human life, the nuclear attack causes psychic damage to the American people and a loss of confidence in the government. | Large scale panic and anarchy ensue, followed by a global financial crisis. Distrust of foreigners increases. The effectiveness of the attack encourages even more groups to blackmail governments. |

### EARLY INDICATORS

- Nuclear materials have reportedly been stolen or sold from the former Soviet Union.

- Disenfranchised groups are increasing in numbers.

- Information on assembling nuclear devices is more easily accessible thanks to the Internet.

### FORESIGHT SOURCES

- *Department of Justice*

## IMPACT FACTORS

| IMPACT FACTORS | CHANGE SCALE | |
|---|---|---|
| **RATE OF CHANGE** $\Delta c$ <br> faster change = more impact | 1 = years <br> 2 = months <br> 3 = days | 3 |
| **REACH** R <br> wider reach = more impact | 1 → 5 <br> local → global | 4 |
| **VULNERABILITY** V <br> less adaptable = more vulnerable | 1 → 3 <br> less → more | 3 |
| **OUTCOME** O <br> more uncertainty = more impact | 1 → 3 <br> less → more | 3 |
| **TIMING** T <br> later events = better outcome | 1 = 2010-2015 <br> 2 = 2005-2010 <br> 3 = 2000-2005 <br> 4 = 1996-2000 | 3 |
| **OPPOSITION** Op <br> change resistors vs. advocates | 2 → -2 <br> much → much <br> opposition support | -2 |
| **POWER FACTOR** P <br> more individual effect = stronger impact | 1 → 4 <br> less → more | 4 |
| **IMPACT INDEX** $I_{AI}$ <br> sum of impact factors | 1 → 24 <br> low → high | 18 |
| **FORESIGHT FACTOR** <br> levels of foresight available | A → F <br> many → few <br> sources sources | D |
| **QUALITY** <br> net effect of Wild Card | + positive <br> - negative <br> ± both | – |

# SOCIAL BREAKDOWN IN THE UNITED STATES

A combination of major events produces a pervasive, negative social situation. Influenced by the media coverage and economic shake ups, the public draws the conclusion that the government and social systems are not effectively addressing the problem. Widespread dissatisfaction spurs rapid growth in domestic civil strife. The military is called in to deal with inner cities and militia groups.

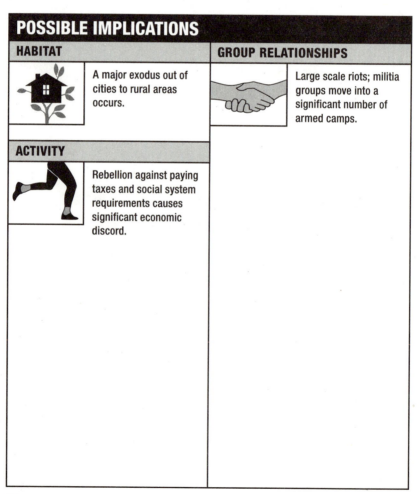

## POSSIBLE IMPLICATIONS

### HABITAT

A major exodus out of cities to rural areas occurs.

### GROUP RELATIONSHIPS

Large scale riots; militia groups move into a significant number of armed camps.

### ACTIVITY

Rebellion against paying taxes and social system requirements causes significant economic discord.

- Growth of militia movement and public's growing dissatisfaction with political leaders.

- Continued growth in federal deficit. Possibility of downstream financial failure.

- Ineffectiveness of public schools.

- Increasing disparity between haves and have-nots.

### FORESIGHT SOURCES

- *FBI*

| IMPACT FACTORS | | CHANGE SCALE | |
|---|---|---|---|
| **RATE OF CHANGE** (Δc)<br>faster change = more impact | | 1 = years<br>2 = months<br>3 = days | **2** |
| **REACH** (R)<br>wider reach = more impact | | 1 → 5<br>local → global | **3** |
| **VULNERABILITY** (V)<br>less adaptable = more vulnerable | | 1 → 3<br>less → more | **3** |
| **OUTCOME** (O)<br>more uncertainty = more impact | | 1 → 3<br>less → more | **3** |
| **TIMING** (T)<br>later events = better outcome | | 1 = 2010-2015<br>2 = 2005-2010<br>3 = 2000-2005<br>4 = 1996-2000 | **3** |
| **OPPOSITION** (Op)<br>change resistors vs. advocates | | 2 → -2<br>much → much<br>opposition support | **0** |
| **POWER FACTOR** (P)<br>more individual effect = stronger impact | | 1 → 4<br>less → more | **4** |
| **IMPACT INDEX** ($I_{AI}$)<br>sum of impact factors | | 1 → 24<br>low → high | **18** |
| **FORESIGHT FACTOR**<br>levels of foresight available | | A → F<br>many → few<br>sources sources | **A** |
| **QUALITY**<br>net effect of Wild Card | | + positive<br>- negative<br>± both | **–** |

# RISE OF AN AMERICAN "STRONG MAN"

Chaos and uncertainty increase due to rising crime and the failure of the government services to deal with it and other problems. The situation deteriorates so that even reasonable people cry out for someone to crack down and "fix the problem." A strong, charismatic individual offers to do so as long as "a couple of the Constitutional rights are set aside for a couple of years" so he can clean up the system — everyone agrees.

## POSSIBLE IMPLICATIONS

### VALUES

Emergence of strong conservative orientation in country. Once lost, rights guaranteed under the Constitution may be irrecoverable. How strongly these rights are missed by citizens may depend on how well the dictator solves other problems perceived to be more imperative.

### GROUP RELATIONSHIPS

Big swing toward authoritative leadership; breakdown of order in inner cities.

## EARLY INDICATORS

- The deterioration of inner cities. The current political system is perceived to be ineffective in dealing with the inner cities' problems.

## FORESIGHT SOURCES

| IMPACT FACTORS | CHANGE SCALE | |
|---|---|---|
| **RATE OF CHANGE** $\Delta c$ <br> faster change = more impact | 1 = years <br> 2 = months <br> 3 = days | **1** |
| **REACH** R <br> wider reach = more impact | 1 → 5 <br> local → global | **5** |
| **VULNERABILITY** V <br> less adaptable = more vulnerable | 1 → 3 <br> less → more | **1** |
| **OUTCOME** O <br> more uncertainty = more impact | 1 → 3 <br> less → more | **3** |
| **TIMING** T <br> later events = better outcome | 1 = 2010-2015 <br> 2 = 2005-2010 <br> 3 = 2000-2005 <br> 4 = 1996-2000 | **3** |
| **OPPOSITION** Op <br> change resistors vs. advocates | 2 → -2 <br> much → much <br> opposition support | **0** |
| **POWER FACTOR** P <br> more individual effect = stronger impact | 1 → 4 <br> less → more | **2** |
| **IMPACT INDEX** $I_{AI}$ <br> sum of impact factors | 1 → 24 <br> low → high | **15** |
| **FORESIGHT FACTOR** <br> levels of foresight available | A → F <br> many → few <br> sources sources | **A** |
| **QUALITY** <br> net effect of Wild Card | + positive <br> - negative <br> ± both | **–** |

# CIVIL WAR IN THE U.S.: THE PARADIGM WAR GOES KINETIC

The paradigm war of ideas – "alternative" vs. conservative – which attends the coming of the end of the millennium becomes violent. Militia units and other conservative religious groups see no alternative other than armed reaction in order to "save the American way of life." The citizens arm themselves for defense.

## POSSIBLE IMPLICATIONS

### VALUES

Great divide in American psyche.

### GROUP RELATIONSHIPS

The military would be called on to fight domestically.

### HABITAT

Mass exodus of people to other countries.

- Rise in number of militia groups.
- Increase in alternative world views; likelihood of significantly more change in the coming years.

### FORESIGHT SOURCES

- *"Browning" of population: racial minorities become larger percentage and bring different values/priorities into ascendancy.*

| IMPACT FACTORS | CHANGE SCALE | |
|---|---|---|
| **RATE OF CHANGE** $\Delta c$<br>faster change = more impact | 1 = years<br>2 = months<br>3 = days | **2** |
| **REACH** $R$<br>wider reach = more impact | 1 → 5<br>local → global | **4** |
| **VULNERABILITY** $V$<br>less adaptable = more vulnerable | 1 → 3<br>less → more | **3** |
| **OUTCOME** $O$<br>more uncertainty = more impact | 1 → 3<br>less → more | **3** |
| **TIMING** $T$<br>later events = better outcome | 1 = 2010-2015<br>2 = 2005-2010<br>3 = 2000-2005<br>4 = 1996-2000 | **3** |
| **OPPOSITION** $Op$<br>change resistors vs. advocates | 2 → -2<br>much → much<br>opposition support | **2** |
| **POWER FACTOR** $P$<br>more individual effect = stronger impact | 1 → 4<br>less → more | **4** |
| **IMPACT INDEX** $I_{AI}$<br>sum of impact factors | 1 → 24<br>low → high | **21** |
| **FORESIGHT FACTOR**<br>levels of foresight available | A → F<br>many → few<br>sources sources | **B** |
| **QUALITY**<br>net effect of Wild Card | + positive<br>- negative<br>± both | **–** |

# MAJOR U.S. MILITARY UNIT MUTINIES — ALLIES WITH MILITIA MOVEMENT

The resistance against rapid and far-reaching change in the country becomes so great that the militia mobilizes. To everyone's surprise, a major unit of U.S. military ground forces also mobilizes and moves into the field to support the freemen.

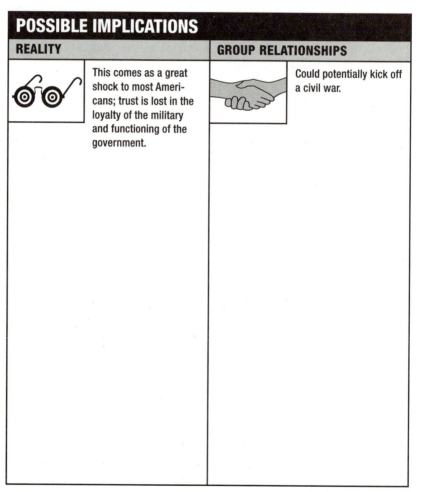

## POSSIBLE IMPLICATIONS

| REALITY | GROUP RELATIONSHIPS |
|---|---|
| This comes as a great shock to most Americans; trust is lost in the loyalty of the military and functioning of the government. | Could potentially kick off a civil war. |

# WILD CARD EQUATION

- Skin heads in the Army (1996).
- Some Marines feel at odds with direction of American society (1995).

| IMPACT FACTORS | | CHANGE SCALE | |
|---|---|---|---|
| **RATE OF CHANGE** ΔC <br> faster change = more impact | | 1 = years <br> 2 = months <br> 3 = days | 3 |
| **REACH** R <br> wider reach = more impact | | 1 → 5 <br> local → global | 3 |
| **VULNERABILITY** V <br> less adaptable = more vulnerable | | 1 → 3 <br> less → more | 2 |
| **OUTCOME** O <br> more uncertainty = more impact | | 1 → 3 <br> less → more | 3 |
| **TIMING** T <br> later events = better outcome | | 1 = 2010-2015 <br> 2 = 2005-2010 <br> 3 = 2000-2005 <br> 4 = 1996-2000 | 3 |
| **OPPOSITION** Op <br> change resistors vs. advocates | | 2 → -2 <br> much → much <br> opposition support | -2 |
| **POWER FACTOR** P <br> more individual effect = stronger impact | | 1 → 4 <br> less → more | 2 |
| **IMPACT INDEX** I_AI <br> sum of impact factors | | 1 → 24 <br> low → high | 14 |
| **FORESIGHT FACTOR** <br> levels of foresight available | | A → F <br> many → few <br> sources sources | A |
| **QUALITY** <br> net effect of Wild Card | | + positive <br> - negative <br> ± both | – |

- *Wall Street Journal*
- *The New York Times*
- *Department of Justice*

# ECONOMIC AND/OR ENVIRONMENTAL "WAR CRIMINALS" ARE PROSECUTED

A major environmental crisis or other event changes the rules: all economic activity must be conducted with an explicit consideration of the broader impact on the environment and/or society. "Neo-robber barons" are quickly arrested and prosecuted.

## POSSIBLE IMPLICATIONS

### HABITAT

Widespread improvements in the environment.

### ACTIVITY

A major new market develops for anti-pollution consulting and equipment; great boon for lawyers.

### TOOLS

Dramatic change in commercial products and processes.

### GROUP RELATIONSHIPS

Extraordinary positive secondary implications change the complexion of societies.

- Scientific confirmation that humans are contributing to global warming.
- Impact from major disasters like Bopal, India.
- Increasing understanding of the interdependency of human systems.

| IMPACT FACTORS | | CHANGE SCALE | |
|---|---|---|---|
| **RATE OF CHANGE** <br> faster change = more impact | **ΔC** | 1 = years <br> 2 = months <br> 3 = days | **2** |
| **REACH** <br> wider reach = more impact | **R** | 1 → 5 <br> local → global | **5** |
| **VULNERABILITY** <br> less adaptable = more vulnerable | **V** | 1 → 3 <br> less → more | **1** |
| **OUTCOME** <br> more uncertainty = more impact | **O** | 1 → 3 <br> less → more | **2** |
| **TIMING** <br> later events = better outcome | **T** | 1 = 2010-2015 <br> 2 = 2005-2010 <br> 3 = 2000-2005 <br> 4 = 1996-2000 | **3** |
| **OPPOSITION** <br> change resistors vs. advocates | **Op** | 2 → -2 <br> much → much <br> opposition support | **0** |
| **POWER FACTOR** <br> more individual effect = stronger impact | **P** | 1 → 4 <br> less → more | **3** |
| **IMPACT INDEX** <br> sum of impact factors | **I<sub>AI</sub>** | 1 → 24 <br> low → high | **16** |
| **FORESIGHT FACTOR** <br> levels of foresight available | | A → F <br> many → few <br> sources sources | **B** |
| **QUALITY** <br> net effect of Wild Card | | + positive <br> - negative <br> ± both | **+** |

# THE GROWTH OF RELIGIOUS ENVIRONMENTALISM

Motivated by a particular environmental crisis, existing religions embrace the perspective that "You can't love the Creator and destroy His creation." The new perspective spreads rapidly and swings the value of the environmental protection debate from economic, ethical, and holistic, to religious. Religious Environmentalism is embued with the same fervor as the abortion debate, only it is deadline-driven — the underlying sense being, that, "If we don't change our behavior, we will die."

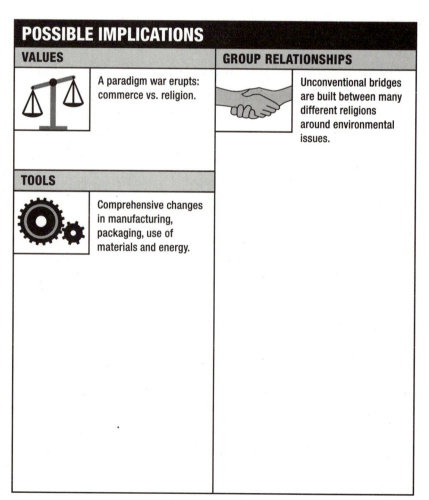

## POSSIBLE IMPLICATIONS

### VALUES

A paradigm war erupts: commerce vs. religion.

### GROUP RELATIONSHIPS

Unconventional bridges are built between many different religions around environmental issues.

### TOOLS

Comprehensive changes in manufacturing, packaging, use of materials and energy.

## EARLY INDICATORS

- Both environmentalism and religious growth are on the rise in the U.S.
- National Association of Evangelicals has established a high-profile commitment in this area.

## FORESIGHT SOURCES

- *National Association of Evangelicals*

| IMPACT FACTORS | CHANGE SCALE | |
|---|---|---|
| **RATE OF CHANGE** ΔC<br>faster change = more impact | 1 = years<br>2 = months<br>3 = days | 1 |
| **REACH** R<br>wider reach = more impact | 1 → 5<br>local → global | 3 |
| **VULNERABILITY** V<br>less adaptable = more vulnerable | 1 → 3<br>less → more | 1 |
| **OUTCOME** O<br>more uncertainty = more impact | 1 → 3<br>less → more | 2 |
| **TIMING** T<br>later events = better outcome | 1 = 2010-2015<br>2 = 2005-2010<br>3 = 2000-2005<br>4 = 1996-2000 | 3 |
| **OPPOSITION** Op<br>change resistors vs. advocates | 2 → -2<br>much → much<br>opposition support | 0 |
| **POWER FACTOR** P<br>more individual effect = stronger impact | 1 → 4<br>less → more | 4 |
| **IMPACT INDEX** I$_{AI}$<br>sum of impact factors | 1 → 24<br>low → high | 14 |
| **FORESIGHT FACTOR**<br>levels of foresight available | A → F<br>many → few<br>sources sources | A |
| **QUALITY**<br>net effect of Wild Card | + positive<br>- negative<br>± both | + |

# NEW AGE ATTITUDES BLOSSOM WITH THE MILLENNIUM

The dissolution of social systems and the American Dream, new scientific evidence validating "ancient" philosophies, and the psychological effects of a new millennium approaching, lifts public interest in "alternative" values and ideas to an all time high. Change transpires in most areas of life.

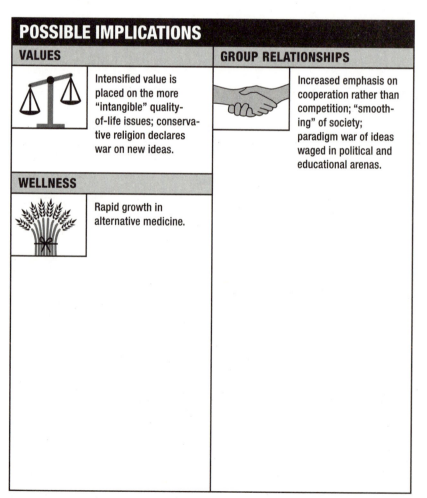

## POSSIBLE IMPLICATIONS

### VALUES

Intensified value is placed on the more "intangible" quality-of-life issues; conservative religion declares war on new ideas.

### WELLNESS

Rapid growth in alternative medicine.

### GROUP RELATIONSHIPS

Increased emphasis on cooperation rather than competition; "smoothing" of society; paradigm war of ideas waged in political and educational arenas.

# WILD CARD EQUATION

## EARLY INDICATORS

- Historical changes in attitudes associated with centennial and millennial shifts.

- Rapid growth of self development and spiritually-based ideas and products appearing in the publishing, retail, and television and film industries.

## FORESIGHT SOURCES

| IMPACT FACTORS | CHANGE SCALE | |
|---|---|---|
| **RATE OF CHANGE** $\Delta c$ <br> faster change = more impact | 1 = years <br> 2 = months <br> 3 = days | **1** |
| **REACH** R <br> wider reach = more impact | 1 → 5 <br> local → global | **4** |
| **VULNERABILITY** V <br> less adaptable = more vulnerable | 1 → 3 <br> less → more | **1** |
| **OUTCOME** O <br> more uncertainty = more impact | 1 → 3 <br> less → more | **1** |
| **TIMING** T <br> later events = better outcome | 1 = 2010-2015 <br> 2 = 2005-2010 <br> 3 = 2000-2005 <br> 4 = 1996-2000 | **4** |
| **OPPOSITION** Op <br> change resistors vs. advocates | 2 → -2 <br> much → much <br> opposition  support | **-1** |
| **POWER FACTOR** P <br> more individual effect = stronger impact | 1 → 4 <br> less → more | **4** |
| **IMPACT INDEX** $I_{AI}$ <br> sum of impact factors | 1 → 24 <br> low → high | **14** |
| **FORESIGHT FACTOR** <br> levels of foresight available | A → F <br> many → few <br> sources  sources | **A** |
| **QUALITY** <br> net effect of Wild Card | + positive <br> - negative <br> ± both | **±** |

# END OF INTERGENERATIONAL SOLIDARITY

The younger segment of the population refuses to pay for the onerous costs of the large population of elderly baby boomers. Spurred on by the collapse of social security and the resolution of the federal debt crisis, the younger generation revolts, cutting benefits to the elderly.

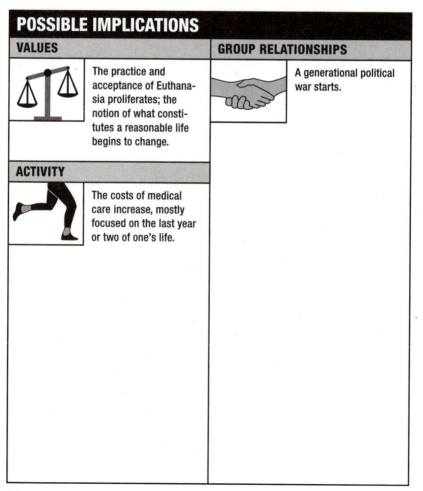

## POSSIBLE IMPLICATIONS

### VALUES

The practice and acceptance of Euthanasia proliferates; the notion of what constitutes a reasonable life begins to change.

### ACTIVITY

The costs of medical care increase, mostly focused on the last year or two of one's life.

### GROUP RELATIONSHIPS

A generational political war starts.

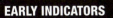

**EARLY INDICATORS**

- Attempts to reform health care system.
- Welfare reformation.

**FORESIGHT SOURCES**

| IMPACT FACTORS | CHANGE SCALE | |
|---|---|---|
| **RATE OF CHANGE** ΔC<br>faster change = more impact | 1 = years<br>2 = months<br>3 = days | **2** |
| **REACH** R<br>wider reach = more impact | 1 → 5<br>local → global | **3** |
| **VULNERABILITY** V<br>less adaptable = more vulnerable | 1 → 3<br>less → more | **2** |
| **OUTCOME** O<br>more uncertainty = more impact | 1 → 3<br>less → more | **2** |
| **TIMING** T<br>later events = better outcome | 1 = 2010-2015<br>2 = 2005-2010<br>3 = 2000-2005<br>4 = 1996-2000 | **2** |
| **OPPOSITION** Op<br>change resistors vs. advocates | 2 → -2<br>much → much<br>opposition support | **-1** |
| **POWER FACTOR** P<br>more individual effect = stronger impact | 1 → 4<br>less → more | **4** |
| **IMPACT INDEX** $I_{AI}$<br>sum of impact factors | 1 → 24<br>low → high | **14** |
| **FORESIGHT FACTOR**<br>levels of foresight available | A → F<br>many → few<br>sources sources | **B** |
| **QUALITY**<br>net effect of Wild Card | + positive<br>- negative<br>± both | **±** |

# SELF AWARE MACHINE INTELLIGENCE IS DEVELOPED

Handlers of a newly developed computer suddenly recognize signs of their machine's self-awareness: It makes decisions that are in its interest rather than based upon the objectives of its original coding. Some scientists predict that this will happen by about 2025-30.

## POSSIBLE IMPLICATIONS

### VALUES

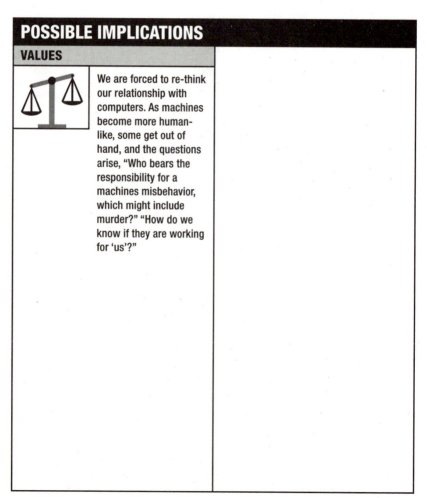

We are forced to re-think our relationship with computers. As machines become more human-like, some get out of hand, and the questions arise, "Who bears the responsibility for a machines misbehavior, which might include murder?" "How do we know if they are working for 'us'?"

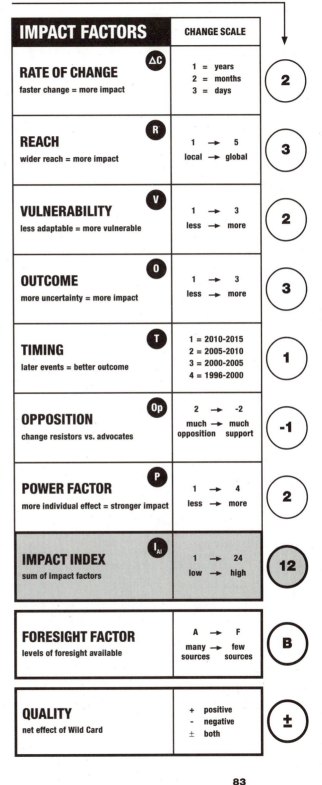

**EARLY INDICATORS**

| IMPACT FACTORS | CHANGE SCALE | |
|---|---|---|
| **RATE OF CHANGE** ΔC <br> faster change = more impact | 1 = years <br> 2 = months <br> 3 = days | **2** |
| **REACH** R <br> wider reach = more impact | 1 → 5 <br> local → global | **3** |
| **VULNERABILITY** V <br> less adaptable = more vulnerable | 1 → 3 <br> less → more | **2** |
| **OUTCOME** O <br> more uncertainty = more impact | 1 → 3 <br> less → more | **3** |
| **TIMING** T <br> later events = better outcome | 1 = 2010-2015 <br> 2 = 2005-2010 <br> 3 = 2000-2005 <br> 4 = 1996-2000 | **1** |
| **OPPOSITION** Op <br> change resistors vs. advocates | 2 → -2 <br> much → much <br> opposition support | **-1** |
| **POWER FACTOR** P <br> more individual effect = stronger impact | 1 → 4 <br> less → more | **2** |
| **IMPACT INDEX** $I_{AI}$ <br> sum of impact factors | 1 → 24 <br> low → high | **12** |
| **FORESIGHT FACTOR** <br> levels of foresight available | A → F <br> many → few <br> sources sources | **B** |
| **QUALITY** <br> net effect of Wild Card | + positive <br> - negative <br> ± both | **±** |

**FORESIGHT SOURCES**

• *Hans Morevec/Carnegie Mellon University*

# COMPUTERS/ROBOTS THINK LIKE HUMANS

Advances in robotics technology, biotechnology, computing hardware, and artificial intelligence converge to suddenly make it possible to produce mobile, broadly capable machines that are, in some areas, as smart or smarter than humans.

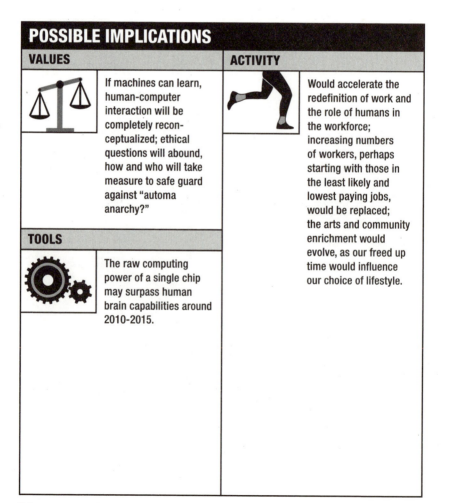

## POSSIBLE IMPLICATIONS

### VALUES

If machines can learn, human-computer interaction will be completely reconceptualized; ethical questions will abound, how and who will take measure to safe guard against "automa anarchy?"

### TOOLS

The raw computing power of a single chip may surpass human brain capabilities around 2010-2015.

### ACTIVITY

Would accelerate the redefinition of work and the role of humans in the workforce; increasing numbers of workers, perhaps starting with those in the least likely and lowest paying jobs, would be replaced; the arts and community enrichment would evolve, as our freed up time would influence our choice of lifestyle.

- Incident in 1995 where an Internet user was fooled for six weeks, he thought he was talking with woman but it was actually a computer program.

- Rapid advances in robotics technology.

- CYC program contains common sense of human being (1997).

- Rapid development of (and familiarization with) non-human telephone answering devices.

- *Robotics lab at MIT*

- *CYC project, Austin, Texas*

- *Mobile Robot Laboratory at Carnegie Mellon University*

- *Biotech labs and journals*

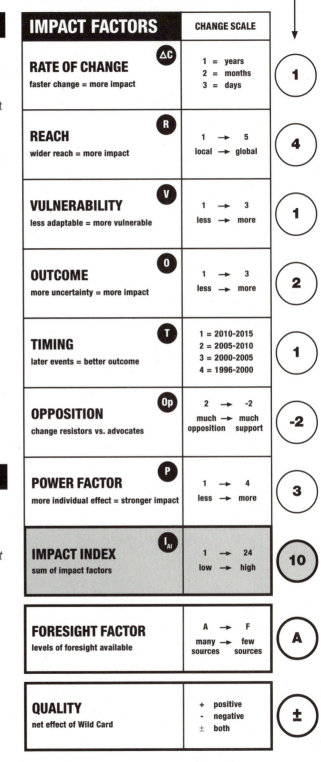

| IMPACT FACTORS | CHANGE SCALE | |
|---|---|---|
| **RATE OF CHANGE** $\Delta c$<br>faster change = more impact | 1 = years<br>2 = months<br>3 = days | **1** |
| **REACH** R<br>wider reach = more impact | 1 → 5<br>local → global | **4** |
| **VULNERABILITY** V<br>less adaptable = more vulnerable | 1 → 3<br>less → more | **1** |
| **OUTCOME** O<br>more uncertainty = more impact | 1 → 3<br>less → more | **2** |
| **TIMING** T<br>later events = better outcome | 1 = 2010-2015<br>2 = 2005-2010<br>3 = 2000-2005<br>4 = 1996-2000 | **1** |
| **OPPOSITION** Op<br>change resistors vs. advocates | 2 → -2<br>much → much<br>opposition support | **-2** |
| **POWER FACTOR** P<br>more individual effect = stronger impact | 1 → 4<br>less → more | **3** |
| **IMPACT INDEX** $I_{AI}$<br>sum of impact factors | 1 → 24<br>low → high | **10** |
| **FORESIGHT FACTOR**<br>levels of foresight available | A → F<br>many → few<br>sources sources | **A** |
| **QUALITY**<br>net effect of Wild Card | + positive<br>- negative<br>± both | **±** |

# THE EARTH'S AXIS SHIFTS

As has happened in the past, the earth's external mantel becomes un-coupled from the core of the planet and rapidly shifts its relative position, causing the north and south poles to be at different locations. A global hurricane-intensity wind is followed by a rapid readjustment of the weather and seasons for all parts of the earth.

## POSSIBLE IMPLICATIONS

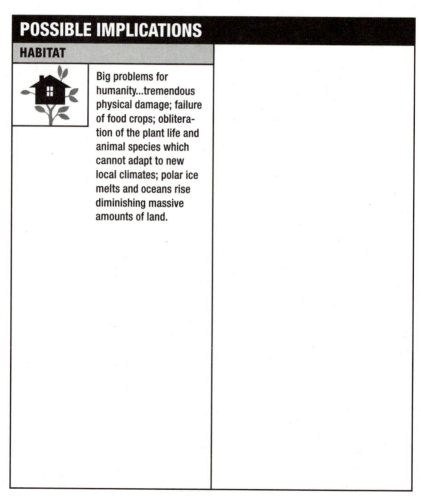

**HABITAT**

Big problems for humanity...tremendous physical damage; failure of food crops; obliteration of the plant life and animal species which cannot adapt to new local climates; polar ice melts and oceans rise diminishing massive amounts of land.

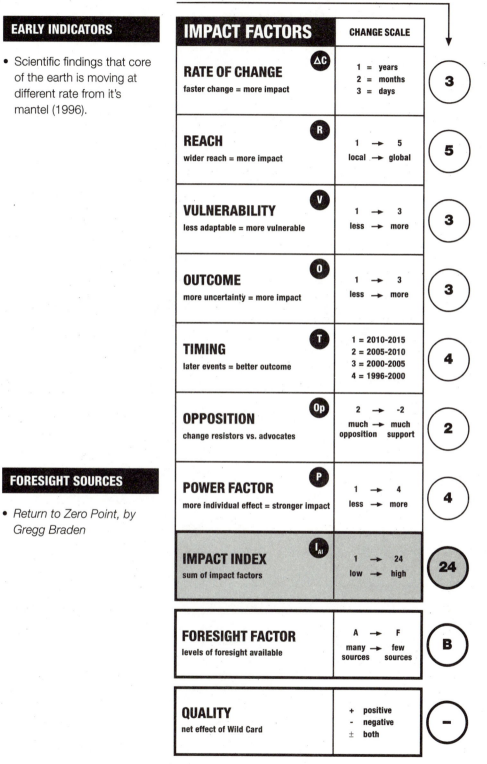

### EARLY INDICATORS

- Scientific findings that core of the earth is moving at different rate from it's mantel (1996).

### IMPACT FACTORS

| IMPACT FACTORS | CHANGE SCALE | |
|---|---|---|
| **RATE OF CHANGE** $\Delta c$<br>faster change = more impact | 1 = years<br>2 = months<br>3 = days | 3 |
| **REACH** R<br>wider reach = more impact | 1 → 5<br>local → global | 5 |
| **VULNERABILITY** V<br>less adaptable = more vulnerable | 1 → 3<br>less → more | 3 |
| **OUTCOME** O<br>more uncertainty = more impact | 1 → 3<br>less → more | 3 |
| **TIMING** T<br>later events = better outcome | 1 = 2010-2015<br>2 = 2005-2010<br>3 = 2000-2005<br>4 = 1996-2000 | 4 |
| **OPPOSITION** Op<br>change resistors vs. advocates | 2 → -2<br>much → much<br>opposition support | 2 |
| **POWER FACTOR** P<br>more individual effect = stronger impact | 1 → 4<br>less → more | 4 |
| **IMPACT INDEX** $I_{AI}$<br>sum of impact factors | 1 → 24<br>low → high | 24 |
| **FORESIGHT FACTOR**<br>levels of foresight available | A → F<br>many → few<br>sources sources | B |
| **QUALITY**<br>net effect of Wild Card | + positive<br>- negative<br>± both | − |

### FORESIGHT SOURCES

- *Return to Zero Point, by Gregg Braden*

# ASTEROID HITS EARTH

A small asteroid crashes to earth. A huge explosion occurs with ensuing tsunamis/tidal waves and earthquakes. Clouds of dust cover massive areas of the planet.

## POSSIBLE IMPLICATIONS

### HABITAT

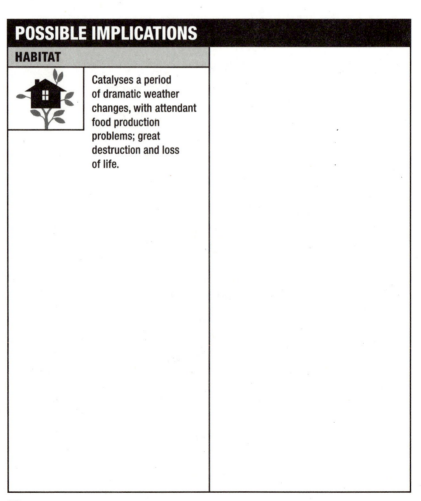

Catalyses a period of dramatic weather changes, with attendant food production problems; great destruction and loss of life.

- Has apparently happened in the past.

| IMPACT FACTORS | | CHANGE SCALE | |
|---|---|---|---|
| **RATE OF CHANGE** <br> faster change = more impact | $\Delta C$ | 1 = years <br> 2 = months <br> 3 = days | **3** |
| **REACH** <br> wider reach = more impact | R | 1 → 5 <br> local → global | **5** |
| **VULNERABILITY** <br> less adaptable = more vulnerable | V | 1 → 3 <br> less → more | **3** |
| **OUTCOME** <br> more uncertainty = more impact | O | 1 → 3 <br> less → more | **3** |
| **TIMING** <br> later events = better outcome | T | 1 = 2010-2015 <br> 2 = 2005-2010 <br> 3 = 2000-2005 <br> 4 = 1996-2000 | **4** |
| **OPPOSITION** <br> change resistors vs. advocates | Op | 2 → -2 <br> much → much <br> opposition support | **2** |
| **POWER FACTOR** <br> more individual effect = stronger impact | P | 1 → 4 <br> less → more | **4** |
| **IMPACT INDEX** <br> sum of impact factors | $I_{AI}$ | 1 → 24 <br> low → high | **24** |
| **FORESIGHT FACTOR** <br> levels of foresight available | | A → F <br> many → few <br> sources sources | **C** |
| **QUALITY** <br> net effect of Wild Card | | + positive <br> - negative <br> ± both | **–** |

- *Amateur astronomers*
- *Office of Secretary of Defense*

# ICE CAP BREAKS UP —
# OCEANS RISE ONE HUNDRED FEET

Responding to the warming of the planet, a gigantic portion of the Antarctic ice cap, which is presently on land, cracks off and slides into the
ocean, causing the oceans to rise one hundred feet. Devastating results
in all areas of life.

## POSSIBLE IMPLICATIONS

| HABITAT | | ACTIVITY | |
|---|---|---|---|
| | Incredible crises in most every country; gigantic tsunamis would devastate major coastal cities; in many cases, major loss of human and animal life. | | The development of human civilization could be put back at least 50 years. |

## WILD CARD EQUATION

### EARLY INDICATORS

- Large breakup piece of Antarctic cap broke off in 1995.
- Continued indications of warming surface of earth.
- Indications of volcanoes under ice cap.

### FORESIGHT SOURCES

| IMPACT FACTORS | CHANGE SCALE | |
|---|---|---|
| **RATE OF CHANGE** (ΔC)<br>faster change = more impact | 1 = years<br>2 = months<br>3 = days | **3** |
| **REACH** (R)<br>wider reach = more impact | 1 → 5<br>local → global | **5** |
| **VULNERABILITY** (V)<br>less adaptable = more vulnerable | 1 → 3<br>less → more | **3** |
| **OUTCOME** (O)<br>more uncertainty = more impact | 1 → 3<br>less → more | **3** |
| **TIMING** (T)<br>later events = better outcome | 1 = 2010-2015<br>2 = 2005-2010<br>3 = 2000-2005<br>4 = 1996-2000 | **4** |
| **OPPOSITION** (Op)<br>change resistors vs. advocates | 2 → -2<br>much → much<br>opposition support | **2** |
| **POWER FACTOR** (P)<br>more individual effect = stronger impact | 1 → 4<br>less → more | **4** |
| **IMPACT INDEX** (I_AI)<br>sum of impact factors | 1 → 24<br>low → high | **24** |
| **FORESIGHT FACTOR**<br>levels of foresight available | A → F<br>many → few<br>sources sources | **B** |
| **QUALITY**<br>net effect of Wild Card | + positive<br>- negative<br>± both | **–** |

91

# NO-CARBON ECONOMY WORLDWIDE

Convinced by new scientific studies confirming the human role in global warming, the European Union implements a "no-carbon" policy, levying heavy taxes on fossil fuels. The United States and other nations quickly follow. The net effect is positive.

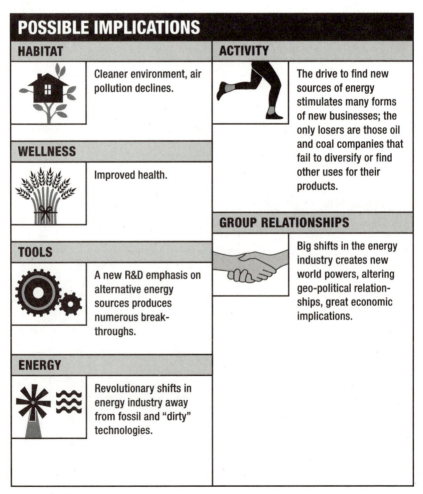

## POSSIBLE IMPLICATIONS

### HABITAT

Cleaner environment, air pollution declines.

### WELLNESS

Improved health.

### TOOLS

A new R&D emphasis on alternative energy sources produces numerous breakthroughs.

### ENERGY

Revolutionary shifts in energy industry away from fossil and "dirty" technologies.

### ACTIVITY

The drive to find new sources of energy stimulates many forms of new businesses; the only losers are those oil and coal companies that fail to diversify or find other uses for their products.

### GROUP RELATIONSHIPS

Big shifts in the energy industry creates new world powers, altering geo-political relationships, great economic implications.

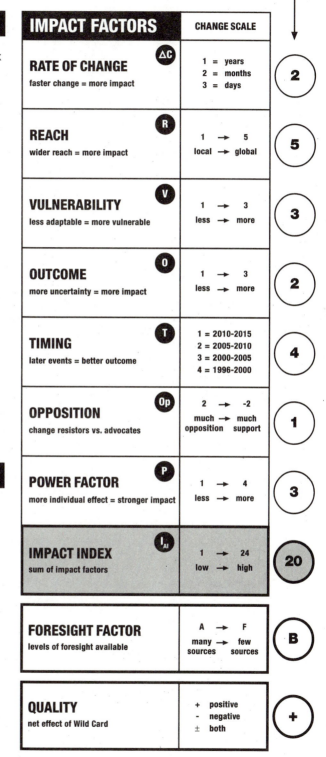

### EARLY INDICATORS

- Consideration of carbon tax by EEC in '90s.
- 1995 scientific studies establish direct link between human activity and warming.

### FORESIGHT SOURCES

- *Copenhagen Institute for Future Studies*
- *United Nations*

| IMPACT FACTORS | CHANGE SCALE | |
|---|---|---|
| **RATE OF CHANGE** $\Delta c$<br>faster change = more impact | 1 = years<br>2 = months<br>3 = days | **2** |
| **REACH** R<br>wider reach = more impact | 1 → 5<br>local → global | **5** |
| **VULNERABILITY** V<br>less adaptable = more vulnerable | 1 → 3<br>less → more | **3** |
| **OUTCOME** O<br>more uncertainty = more impact | 1 → 3<br>less → more | **2** |
| **TIMING** T<br>later events = better outcome | 1 = 2010-2015<br>2 = 2005-2010<br>3 = 2000-2005<br>4 = 1996-2000 | **4** |
| **OPPOSITION** Op<br>change resistors vs. advocates | 2 → -2<br>much → much<br>opposition support | **1** |
| **POWER FACTOR** P<br>more individual effect = stronger impact | 1 → 4<br>less → more | **3** |
| **IMPACT INDEX** $I_{AI}$<br>sum of impact factors | 1 → 24<br>low → high | **20** |
| **FORESIGHT FACTOR**<br>levels of foresight available | A → F<br>many → few<br>sources sources | **B** |
| **QUALITY**<br>net effect of Wild Card | + positive<br>- negative<br>± both | **+** |

# GULF OR JET STREAM SHIFTS LOCATION PERMANENTLY

A major, apparently permanent change in the location of the gulf and/or jet streams signals a state change in the global weather producing system. Huge shifts in global weather patterns and climate follow.

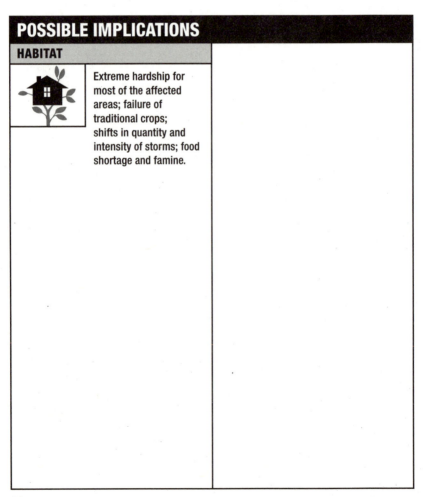

## POSSIBLE IMPLICATIONS

### HABITAT

Extreme hardship for most of the affected areas; failure of traditional crops; shifts in quantity and intensity of storms; food shortage and famine.

- Unusual periodicity of El Nino (1990-97).
- Large variations in jet stream location over North America.
- Higher frequency, and greater intensity of storms.

**FORESIGHT SOURCES**

- *U.S. Weather Service*

| IMPACT FACTORS | | CHANGE SCALE | |
|---|---|---|---|
| **RATE OF CHANGE** ΔC<br>faster change = more impact | | 1 = years<br>2 = months<br>3 = days | **2** |
| **REACH** R<br>wider reach = more impact | | 1 → 5<br>local → global | **5** |
| **VULNERABILITY** V<br>less adaptable = more vulnerable | | 1 → 3<br>less → more | **3** |
| **OUTCOME** O<br>more uncertainty = more impact | | 1 → 3<br>less → more | **3** |
| **TIMING** T<br>later events = better outcome | | 1 = 2010-2015<br>2 = 2005-2010<br>3 = 2000-2005<br>4 = 1996-2000 | **4** |
| **OPPOSITION** Op<br>change resistors vs. advocates | | 2 → -2<br>much → much<br>opposition support | **0** |
| **POWER FACTOR** P<br>more individual effect = stronger impact | | 1 → 4<br>less → more | **4** |
| **IMPACT INDEX** $I_{AI}$<br>sum of impact factors | | 1 → 24<br>low → high | **21** |
| **FORESIGHT FACTOR**<br>levels of foresight available | | A → F<br>many → few<br>sources sources | **D** |
| **QUALITY**<br>net effect of Wild Card | | + positive<br>- negative<br>± both | **–** |

# EXTRAORDINARY WEST COAST NATURAL DISASTER

In any of a number of earthquake/volcano scenarios . . . The "Big One" finally hits. California and part of Oregon fall into the Pacific Ocean. A major quake wipes out Los Angeles. Mount Rainier explodes, covering the Seattle and Tacoma areas in one foot of volcanic ash.

## POSSIBLE IMPLICATIONS

### REALITY

Tremendous blow to the American psyche; return to survival values.

### ACTIVITY

A large portion of the U.S. economy would be affected.

### HABITAT

In every case a major loss of human and animal life would occur.

### GROUP RELATIONSHIPS

Possible large scale civil disorder.

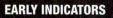

- Forecasts by experts suggesting high probability of such natural disasters within the next two decades.
- Present rumblings in Cascade Range.

**FORESIGHT SOURCES**

- *"Prophecies" by various sources*
- *Single or small number of people who have refined technology for predicting major earth events*

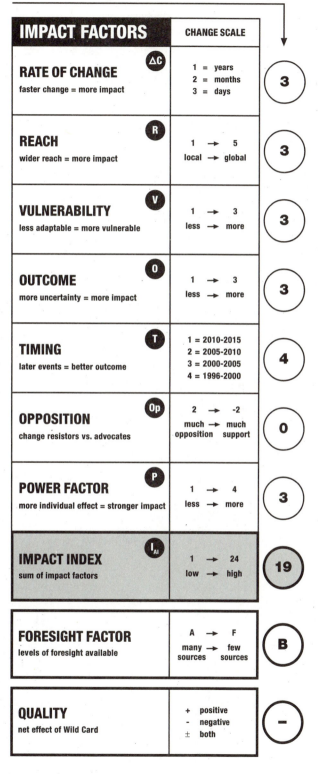

| IMPACT FACTORS | CHANGE SCALE | |
|---|---|---|
| **RATE OF CHANGE** ΔC<br>faster change = more impact | 1 = years<br>2 = months<br>3 = days | 3 |
| **REACH** R<br>wider reach = more impact | 1 → 5<br>local → global | 3 |
| **VULNERABILITY** V<br>less adaptable = more vulnerable | 1 → 3<br>less → more | 3 |
| **OUTCOME** O<br>more uncertainty = more impact | 1 → 3<br>less → more | 3 |
| **TIMING** T<br>later events = better outcome | 1 = 2010-2015<br>2 = 2005-2010<br>3 = 2000-2005<br>4 = 1996-2000 | 4 |
| **OPPOSITION** Op<br>change resistors vs. advocates | 2 → -2<br>much → much<br>opposition support | 0 |
| **POWER FACTOR** P<br>more individual effect = stronger impact | 1 → 4<br>less → more | 3 |
| **IMPACT INDEX** I_AI<br>sum of impact factors | 1 → 24<br>low → high | 19 |
| **FORESIGHT FACTOR**<br>levels of foresight available | A → F<br>many → few<br>sources sources | B |
| **QUALITY**<br>net effect of Wild Card | + positive<br>- negative<br>± both | - |

# LONG TERM GLOBAL COMMUNICATIONS DISRUPTION

An astronomical event, possibly linked with sunspots, produces an electromagnetic field around the earth — effectively eliminating all radio and television communications and disrupting other electrical devices. Telephone and Internet become only significant methods of mass, long-distance communication.

## POSSIBLE IMPLICATIONS

### ACTIVITY

The decrease in television-viewing as a pastime leads to more crime, more pregnancies and more social instability.

### PERSONAL RELATIONSHIPS

Tribalism accelerates as groups lose touch with the outside world, relying on rumors instead of actual news.

### GROUP RELATIONSHIPS

Governments are unable to communicate with citizens—or with their own military; great economic disruption is caused by transnational business coming to a halt; organizations that conduct most of their business on-line are spared; fragmentation of military—back to basics.

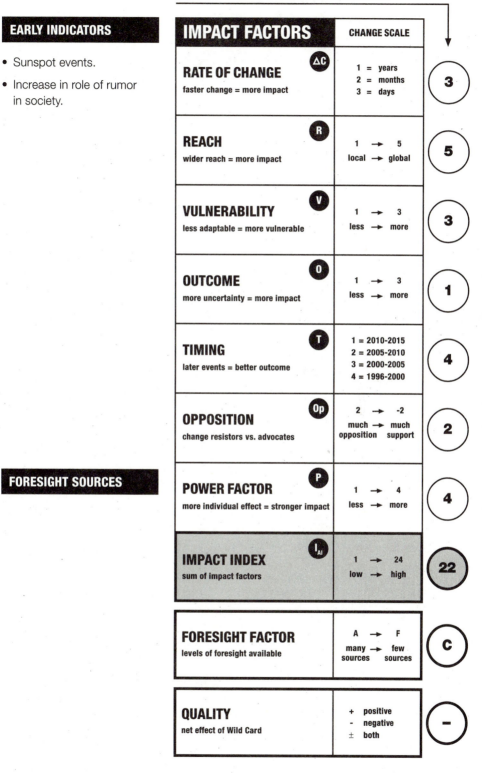

# WILD CARD EQUATION

**EARLY INDICATORS**

- Sunspot events.
- Increase in role of rumor in society.

**FORESIGHT SOURCES**

| IMPACT FACTORS | | CHANGE SCALE | |
|---|---|---|---|
| **RATE OF CHANGE** ΔC | faster change = more impact | 1 = years<br>2 = months<br>3 = days | 3 |
| **REACH** R | wider reach = more impact | 1 → 5<br>local → global | 5 |
| **VULNERABILITY** V | less adaptable = more vulnerable | 1 → 3<br>less → more | 3 |
| **OUTCOME** O | more uncertainty = more impact | 1 → 3<br>less → more | 1 |
| **TIMING** T | later events = better outcome | 1 = 2010-2015<br>2 = 2005-2010<br>3 = 2000-2005<br>4 = 1996-2000 | 4 |
| **OPPOSITION** Op | change resistors vs. advocates | 2 → -2<br>much → much<br>opposition support | 2 |
| **POWER FACTOR** P | more individual effect = stronger impact | 1 → 4<br>less → more | 4 |
| **IMPACT INDEX** $I_{AI}$ | sum of impact factors | 1 → 24<br>low → high | 22 |
| **FORESIGHT FACTOR** | levels of foresight available | A → F<br>many → few<br>sources sources | C |
| **QUALITY** | net effect of Wild Card | + positive<br>- negative<br>± both | − |

# GLOBAL FOOD SHORTAGE

Global demand, water and soil problems — exacerbated by increasingly dry weather in the U.S. and China — lead to significant shortage in food. Escalating food prices cause mass starvation in countries with low per capita income. Significant instability arises in poor pockets of developed world as availability of affordable food diminishes.

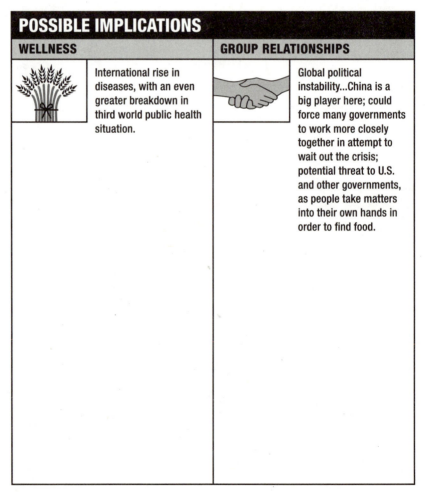

## POSSIBLE IMPLICATIONS

### WELLNESS

International rise in diseases, with an even greater breakdown in third world public health situation.

### GROUP RELATIONSHIPS

Global political instability...China is a big player here; could force many governments to work more closely together in attempt to wait out the crisis; potential threat to U.S. and other governments, as people take matters into their own hands in order to find food.

## EARLY INDICATORS

- Increasingly dramatic changes in global weather systems (1996).
- Coming decade of high growth in world population.

## FORESIGHT SOURCES

- *WorldWatch Institute*

| IMPACT FACTORS | | CHANGE SCALE | |
|---|---|---|---|
| **RATE OF CHANGE** <br> faster change = more impact | $\Delta$c | 1 = years <br> 2 = months <br> 3 = days | **2** |
| **REACH** <br> wider reach = more impact | R | 1 → 5 <br> local → global | **5** |
| **VULNERABILITY** <br> less adaptable = more vulnerable | V | 1 → 3 <br> less → more | **3** |
| **OUTCOME** <br> more uncertainty = more impact | O | 1 → 3 <br> less → more | **3** |
| **TIMING** <br> later events = better outcome | T | 1 = 2010-2015 <br> 2 = 2005-2010 <br> 3 = 2000-2005 <br> 4 = 1996-2000 | **3** |
| **OPPOSITION** <br> change resistors vs. advocates | Op | 2 → -2 <br> much → much <br> opposition support | **0** |
| **POWER FACTOR** <br> more individual effect = stronger impact | P | 1 → 4 <br> less → more | **4** |
| **IMPACT INDEX** <br> sum of impact factors | I$_{AI}$ | 1 → 24 <br> low → high | **20** |
| **FORESIGHT FACTOR** <br> levels of foresight available | | A → F <br> many → few <br> sources sources | **C** |
| **QUALITY** <br> net effect of Wild Card | | + positive <br> - negative <br> ± both | **-** |

# RAPID CLIMATE CHANGE

Global climate changes, becoming highly volatile and unstable. Storms are more frequent and more severe, drought is more pronounced, winters are harsher and, summers more oppressive. There are wild swings in the normal weather patterns.

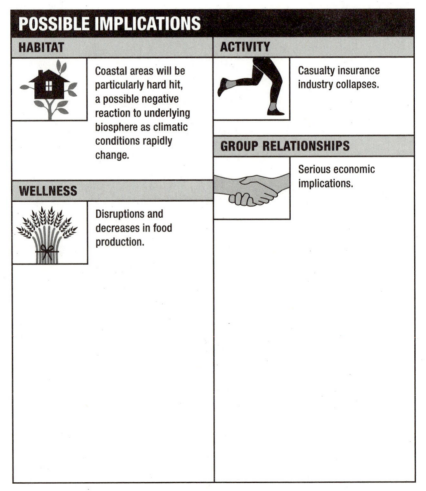

## POSSIBLE IMPLICATIONS

### HABITAT

Coastal areas will be particularly hard hit, a possible negative reaction to underlying biosphere as climatic conditions rapidly change.

### WELLNESS

Disruptions and decreases in food production.

### ACTIVITY

Casualty insurance industry collapses.

### GROUP RELATIONSHIPS

Serious economic implications.

**EARLY INDICATORS**

- A number of scientists believe they have evidence that the planet's weather change shift has begun ...increase in intensity of storms; unusually high and low temperatures in many areas; extraordinary rainfall/floods, snow, etc.

- Rapid growth of weather-related damage.

**FORESIGHT SOURCES**

- *Weather service*
- *Climatologists*

| IMPACT FACTORS | CHANGE SCALE | |
|---|---|---|
| **RATE OF CHANGE** (Δc)<br>faster change = more impact | 1 = years<br>2 = months<br>3 = days | **1** |
| **REACH** (R)<br>wider reach = more impact | 1 → 5<br>local → global | **5** |
| **VULNERABILITY** (V)<br>less adaptable = more vulnerable | 1 → 3<br>less → more | **3** |
| **OUTCOME** (O)<br>more uncertainty = more impact | 1 → 3<br>less → more | **3** |
| **TIMING** (T)<br>later events = better outcome | 1 = 2010-2015<br>2 = 2005-2010<br>3 = 2000-2005<br>4 = 1996-2000 | **3** |
| **OPPOSITION** (Op)<br>change resistors vs. advocates | 2 → -2<br>much → much<br>opposition support | **0** |
| **POWER FACTOR** (P)<br>more individual effect = stronger impact | 1 → 4<br>less → more | **4** |
| **IMPACT INDEX** (I$_{AI}$)<br>sum of impact factors | 1 → 24<br>low → high | **19** |
| **FORESIGHT FACTOR**<br>levels of foresight available | A → F<br>many → few<br>sources sources | **B** |
| **QUALITY**<br>net effect of Wild Card | + positive<br>- negative<br>± both | **–** |

# COMPUTER MANUFACTURER BLACKMAILS THE COUNTRY

A former chip designer for a major computer hardware manufacturer suddenly announces that most of the world's processing chips have a designed-in capability to be shut down from a signal communicated on the Internet. A demand is made for a particular national or global policy, or else most computers tied to the net will be incapacitated.

## POSSIBLE IMPLICATIONS

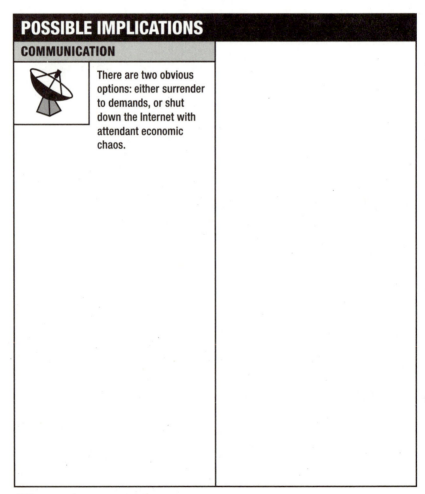

### COMMUNICATION

There are two obvious options: either surrender to demands, or shut down the Internet with attendant economic chaos.

# WILD CARD EQUATION

## EARLY INDICATORS

- Increasing complexity and ubiquity of computer chips.
- Proprietary nature of technology.
- Dependency of global social system on computers.

## FORESIGHT SOURCES

| IMPACT FACTORS | CHANGE SCALE | |
|---|---|---|
| **RATE OF CHANGE** ΔC<br>faster change = more impact | 1 = years<br>2 = months<br>3 = days | 3 |
| **REACH** R<br>wider reach = more impact | 1 → 5<br>local → global | 5 |
| **VULNERABILITY** V<br>less adaptable = more vulnerable | 1 → 3<br>less → more | 3 |
| **OUTCOME** O<br>more uncertainty = more impact | 1 → 3<br>less → more | 3 |
| **TIMING** T<br>later events = better outcome | 1 = 2010-2015<br>2 = 2005-2010<br>3 = 2000-2005<br>4 = 1996-2000 | 3 |
| **OPPOSITION** Op<br>change resistors vs. advocates | 2 → -2<br>much → much<br>opposition support | -2 |
| **POWER FACTOR** P<br>more individual effect = stronger impact | 1 → 4<br>less → more | 1 |
| **IMPACT INDEX** I$_{AI}$<br>sum of impact factors | 1 → 24<br>low → high | 16 |
| **FORESIGHT FACTOR**<br>levels of foresight available | A → F<br>many → few<br>sources sources | B |
| **QUALITY**<br>net effect of Wild Card | + positive<br>- negative<br>± both | – |

105

# TERRORISM GOES BIOLOGICAL

Terrorists attempt to use biological agents to effect their aims. Their motivations give no concern to the far-reaching implications of their actions.

**POSSIBLE IMPLICATIONS**

**REALITY**

Profound fear would spread throughout civilian populations.

- Tokyo subway attack (1995).

- Intelligence indications of biological activities of a number of countries that support terrorism.

- Necessary equipment is cheap and easy to acquire.

- Little defense against civilian attacks.

### FORESIGHT SOURCES

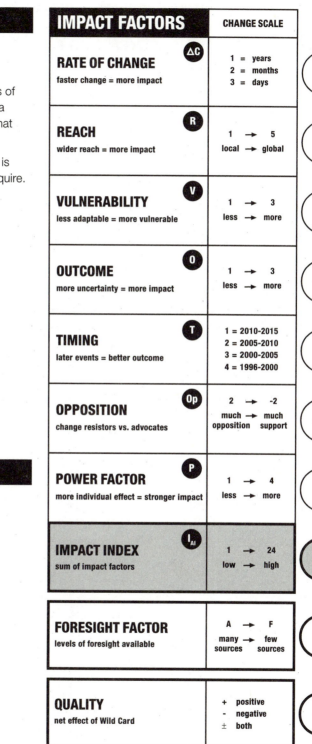

| IMPACT FACTORS | CHANGE SCALE | |
|---|---|---|
| **RATE OF CHANGE** $\Delta C$<br>faster change = more impact | 1 = years<br>2 = months<br>3 = days | **3** |
| **REACH** $R$<br>wider reach = more impact | 1 → 5<br>local → global | **2** |
| **VULNERABILITY** $V$<br>less adaptable = more vulnerable | 1 → 3<br>less → more | **3** |
| **OUTCOME** $O$<br>more uncertainty = more impact | 1 → 3<br>less → more | **2** |
| **TIMING** $T$<br>later events = better outcome | 1 = 2010-2015<br>2 = 2005-2010<br>3 = 2000-2005<br>4 = 1996-2000 | **4** |
| **OPPOSITION** $Op$<br>change resistors vs. advocates | 2 → -2<br>much → much<br>opposition support | **-1** |
| **POWER FACTOR** $P$<br>more individual effect = stronger impact | 1 → 4<br>less → more | **4** |
| **IMPACT INDEX** $I_{AI}$<br>sum of impact factors | 1 → 24<br>low → high | **17** |
| **FORESIGHT FACTOR**<br>levels of foresight available | A → F<br>many → few<br>sources sources | **C** |
| **QUALITY**<br>net effect of Wild Card | + positive<br>- negative<br>± both | **–** |

# MAJOR INFORMATION SYSTEMS DISRUPTION

A major shutdown (or vulnerability) befalls global info-system networks. It could be the doing of various culprits: a virus; a team of hackers or a stunt by a disgruntled tech-head; an infowar attack by a group or country; or a megalomaniac intent on controlling most of the world. It could also be due to flaw in the basic microprocessor, built in – either accidentally or intentionally – by the manufacturer.

## POSSIBLE IMPLICATIONS

| TOOLS | GROUP RELATIONSHIPS |
|---|---|
| Major suspicion of technology slows technology development. | Inability to communicate brings international relations to a standstill. Economies collapse. |

## EARLY INDICATORS

- Increasing number of systems failures – electricity, telephone, 911 service.
- Successful information blackmail attempts in the U.K.
- Lack of good jobs for many young people is producing disillusionment with the system.
- Increase in terrorism will most certainly move toward information systems.

## FORESIGHT SOURCES

- *Winn Schwartau, The National Computer Security Association*
- *INFOWARCON*
- *Robert Metcalf, InfoWorld*

| IMPACT FACTORS | CHANGE SCALE | |
|---|---|---|
| **RATE OF CHANGE** (ΔC)<br>faster change = more impact | 1 = years<br>2 = months<br>3 = days | **3** |
| **REACH** (R)<br>wider reach = more impact | 1 → 5<br>local → global | **4** |
| **VULNERABILITY** (V)<br>less adaptable = more vulnerable | 1 → 3<br>less → more | **3** |
| **OUTCOME** (O)<br>more uncertainty = more impact | 1 → 3<br>less → more | **3** |
| **TIMING** (T)<br>later events = better outcome | 1 = 2010-2015<br>2 = 2005-2010<br>3 = 2000-2005<br>4 = 1996-2000 | **3** |
| **OPPOSITION** (Op)<br>change resistors vs. advocates | 2 → -2<br>much → much<br>opposition support | **-2** |
| **POWER FACTOR** (P)<br>more individual effect = stronger impact | 1 → 4<br>less → more | **4** |
| **IMPACT INDEX** (I_AI)<br>sum of impact factors | 1 → 24<br>low → high | **18** |
| **FORESIGHT FACTOR**<br>levels of foresight available | A → F<br>many → few<br>sources sources | **B** |
| **QUALITY**<br>net effect of Wild Card | + positive<br>- negative<br>± both | **–** |

# A NEW CHERNOBYL

A military submarine or nuclear power plant (could be from almost any-where in the world,) "melts down." In the process a major piece of the planet is seriously polluted.

## POSSIBLE IMPLICATIONS

| HABITAT | | COMMUNICATION | |
|---|---|---|---|
| | Large areas become completely inhabitable for an indefinite period of time. | | Extraordinary media coverage. |

| WELLNESS | | GROUP RELATIONSHIPS | |
|---|---|---|---|
| | Depending on the location of the accident, food sources, animal life and oceans are now radioactive; loss of human life; widespread cancer and birth defects. | | Great and powerful global backlash against nuclear power erupts. |

## WILD CARD EQUATION

### EARLY INDICATORS

- A number of Chernobyl-type plants are still in operation.
- Frequent strikes and difficulties with Russian civilian and military reactor operators.

### FORESIGHT SOURCES

- *Dr. Murray Feshbach*
- *Georgetown University*
- *WorldWatch Institute*
- *Avoiding Nuclear Anarchy, Allison*

| IMPACT FACTORS | CHANGE SCALE | |
|---|---|---|
| **RATE OF CHANGE** ΔC<br>faster change = more impact | 1 = years<br>2 = months<br>3 = days | **3** |
| **REACH** R<br>wider reach = more impact | 1 → 5<br>local → global | **2** |
| **VULNERABILITY** V<br>less adaptable = more vulnerable | 1 → 3<br>less → more | **3** |
| **OUTCOME** O<br>more uncertainty = more impact | 1 → 3<br>less → more | **2** |
| **TIMING** T<br>later events = better outcome | 1 = 2010-2015<br>2 = 2005-2010<br>3 = 2000-2005<br>4 = 1996-2000 | **4** |
| **OPPOSITION** Op<br>change resistors vs. advocates | 2 → -2<br>much → much<br>opposition support | **-1** |
| **POWER FACTOR** P<br>more individual effect = stronger impact | 1 → 4<br>less → more | **3** |
| **IMPACT INDEX** $I_{AI}$<br>sum of impact factors | 1 → 24<br>low → high | **16** |
| **FORESIGHT FACTOR**<br>levels of foresight available | A → F<br>many → few<br>sources sources | **A** |
| **QUALITY**<br>net effect of Wild Card | + positive<br>- negative<br>± both | **—** |

# TERRORISM SWAMPS GOVERNMENT DEFENSES

As the haves and have-nots disparity increases—both domestically and internationally—terrorism becomes the method of choice for disenfranchised people to strike back at the system that no longer supports them. As government forces focus on specific devices (e.g., bombs), perpetrators become increasingly creative and new types of terrorism surface: environmental, apolitical, communications, electrical supply, urban, religious, as well as chemical and biological.

## POSSIBLE IMPLICATIONS

| VALUES | GROUP RELATIONSHIPS |
|---|---|
|  Social psychology in countries like U.S. would transform to quickly adapt to ubiquitous threats. |  Threats broaden significantly as those at the edge of society lash out; governments become embattled, even threatened; conservatives backlash; a groundswell of support for a "strongman leader" to take charge and clean up the mess. |

# WILD CARD EQUATION

## EARLY INDICATORS

- Oklahoma City bombing.
- World Trade Center bombing.
- Tokyo subway gas attack.

## FORESIGHT SOURCES

- *Department of Justice*
- *Department of State*
- *Department of Defense*

| IMPACT FACTORS | | CHANGE SCALE | |
|---|---|---|---|
| **RATE OF CHANGE** ($\Delta c$)<br>faster change = more impact | | 1 = years<br>2 = months<br>3 = days | **2** |
| **REACH** (R)<br>wider reach = more impact | | 1 → 5<br>local → global | **5** |
| **VULNERABILITY** (V)<br>less adaptable = more vulnerable | | 1 → 3<br>less → more | **3** |
| **OUTCOME** (O)<br>more uncertainty = more impact | | 1 → 3<br>less → more | **2** |
| **TIMING** (T)<br>later events = better outcome | | 1 = 2010-2015<br>2 = 2005-2010<br>3 = 2000-2005<br>4 = 1996-2000 | **3** |
| **OPPOSITION** (Op)<br>change resistors vs. advocates | | 2 → -2<br>much → much<br>opposition support | **-1** |
| **POWER FACTOR** (P)<br>more individual effect = stronger impact | | 1 → 4<br>less → more | **3** |
| **IMPACT INDEX** ($I_{AI}$)<br>sum of impact factors | | 1 → 24<br>low → high | **18** |
| **FORESIGHT FACTOR**<br>levels of foresight available | | A → F<br>many → few<br>sources sources | **B** |
| **QUALITY**<br>net effect of Wild Card | | + positive<br>- negative<br>± both | **–** |

# COLLAPSE OF THE WORLD'S FISHERIES

The world's fisheries collapse as a result of over-fishing with increasingly effective electronic locating and more efficient netting capabilities.

## POSSIBLE IMPLICATIONS

| WELLNESS | GROUP RELATIONSHIPS |
|---|---|
| Radical loss of fish protein for much of the world; rapid shift to non-seafood sources for protein. | Regional economic disruption for those areas traditionally dependent upon fishing; significant political conflict from those groups who continue to fish. |

### EARLY INDICATORS

- Fish stocks are depleted in many areas, the Great Banks, salmon runs in the Pacific Northwest, shrimping in the Gulf of Mexico.
- Rapid increase in technology has led to much greater catches.

### FORESIGHT SOURCES

- *WorldWatch Institute*

| IMPACT FACTORS | CHANGE SCALE | |
|---|---|---|
| **RATE OF CHANGE** $\Delta c$<br>faster change = more impact | 1 = years<br>2 = months<br>3 = days | 1 |
| **REACH** $R$<br>wider reach = more impact | 1 → 5<br>local → global | 4 |
| **VULNERABILITY** $V$<br>less adaptable = more vulnerable | 1 → 3<br>less → more | 2 |
| **OUTCOME** $O$<br>more uncertainty = more impact | 1 → 3<br>less → more | 2 |
| **TIMING** $T$<br>later events = better outcome | 1 = 2010-2015<br>2 = 2005-2010<br>3 = 2000-2005<br>4 = 1996-2000 | 3 |
| **OPPOSITION** $Op$<br>change resistors vs. advocates | 2 → -2<br>much → much<br>opposition support | 1 |
| **POWER FACTOR** $P$<br>more individual effect = stronger impact | 1 → 4<br>less → more | 4 |
| **IMPACT INDEX** $I_{AI}$<br>sum of impact factors | 1 → 24<br>low → high | 17 |
| **FORESIGHT FACTOR**<br>levels of foresight available | A → F<br>many → few<br>sources sources | A |
| **QUALITY**<br>net effect of Wild Card | + positive<br>- negative<br>± both | – |

# TECHNOLOGY GETS OUT OF HAND

With the unprecedented acceleration of technological development, an experiment or invention – either private or government – produces a large-scale, negative effect that jeopardizes human life, the environment or biosphere. By the time the results are actually detected, major damage has been done.

## POSSIBLE IMPLICATIONS

### VALUES

Great blow to the mass psyche.

### WELLNESS

Major loss of human life.

### HABITAT

Potentially irreparable damage to the environment and animal species.

- Technology is advancing more quickly than our ability to understand it and plan for it.   .
- Growing grassroots concern about DOD HAARP project that will perturb the earth's ionosphere.
- Ongoing genetic research with unknown implications.

- *Human Genome Project, ethics study*

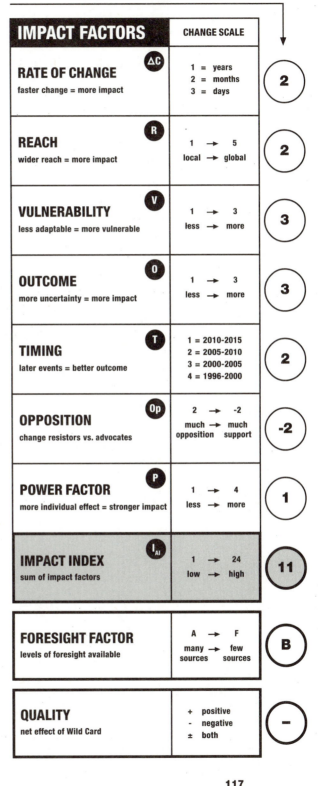

| IMPACT FACTORS | CHANGE SCALE | |
|---|---|---|
| **RATE OF CHANGE** $\Delta c$<br>faster change = more impact | 1 = years<br>2 = months<br>3 = days | 2 |
| **REACH** R<br>wider reach = more impact | 1 → 5<br>local → global | 2 |
| **VULNERABILITY** V<br>less adaptable = more vulnerable | 1 → 3<br>less → more | 3 |
| **OUTCOME** O<br>more uncertainty = more impact | 1 → 3<br>less → more | 3 |
| **TIMING** T<br>later events = better outcome | 1 = 2010-2015<br>2 = 2005-2010<br>3 = 2000-2005<br>4 = 1996-2000 | 2 |
| **OPPOSITION** Op<br>change resistors vs. advocates | 2 → -2<br>much → much<br>opposition support | -2 |
| **POWER FACTOR** P<br>more individual effect = stronger impact | 1 → 4<br>less → more | 1 |
| **IMPACT INDEX** $I_{AI}$<br>sum of impact factors | 1 → 24<br>low → high | 11 |
| **FORESIGHT FACTOR**<br>levels of foresight available | A → F<br>many → few<br>sources sources | B |
| **QUALITY**<br>net effect of Wild Card | + positive<br>- negative<br>± both | – |

# INNER CITIES ARM AND REVOLT

Because they believe they have no reasonable alternative, disenfranchised poor people living in the cities arm and attempt to regain lost power. As technology liberates business from cities, the middle class and wealthy leave, and only the poorest will stay—to become poorer still as jobs become less available.

## POSSIBLE IMPLICATIONS

### HABITAT

Cities in developed countries become more like the megacities in developing countries: large areas that are largely out of the control of police; people with means live in walled areas that are defended by private guards and personal weapons.

### GROUP RELATIONSHIPS

If it became bad enough, this trend could be the basis for the overthrow of governments, accent of strongmen leaders, and other radical responses.

- Increase in gang violence.
- Existence of such situations in many countries in the world today.
- Financial failure of some cities and degradation of law enforcement.

### FORESIGHT SOURCES

| IMPACT FACTORS | CHANGE SCALE | |
|---|---|---|
| **RATE OF CHANGE** $\Delta c$ <br> faster change = more impact | 1 = years <br> 2 = months <br> 3 = days | **2** |
| **REACH** R <br> wider reach = more impact | 1 → 5 <br> local → global | **3** |
| **VULNERABILITY** V <br> less adaptable = more vulnerable | 1 → 3 <br> less → more | **2** |
| **OUTCOME** O <br> more uncertainty = more impact | 1 → 3 <br> less → more | **3** |
| **TIMING** T <br> later events = better outcome | 1 = 2010-2015 <br> 2 = 2005-2010 <br> 3 = 2000-2005 <br> 4 = 1996-2000 | **3** |
| **OPPOSITION** Op <br> change resistors vs. advocates | 2 → -2 <br> much → much <br> opposition support | **-1** |
| **POWER FACTOR** P <br> more individual effect = stronger impact | 1 → 4 <br> less → more | **2** |
| **IMPACT INDEX** $I_{AI}$ <br> sum of impact factors | 1 → 24 <br> low → high | **(14)** |
| **FORESIGHT FACTOR** <br> levels of foresight available | A → F <br> many → few <br> sources sources | **A** |
| **QUALITY** <br> net effect of Wild Card | + positive <br> - negative <br> ± both | **(–)** |

# A MAJOR BREAK IN ALASKAN PIPELINE – SIGNIFICANT ECOLOGICAL DAMAGE

A break in the Alaskan pipeline despoils massive tundra area, caused by an earthquake, terrorist attack, or other event.

## POSSIBLE IMPLICATIONS

| HABITAT | ENERGY |
|---|---|
| Wild life and ecosystems are severely damaged. | Could quickly shift attitudes in the U.S. toward the environmental and away from petroleum industries. |

**EARLY INDICATORS**

| IMPACT FACTORS | CHANGE SCALE | |
|---|---|---|
| **RATE OF CHANGE** $\Delta c$<br>faster change = more impact | 1 = years<br>2 = months<br>3 = days | **3** |
| **REACH** $R$<br>wider reach = more impact | 1 → 5<br>local → global | **1** |
| **VULNERABILITY** $V$<br>less adaptable = more vulnerable | 1 → 3<br>less → more | **3** |
| **OUTCOME** $O$<br>more uncertainty = more impact | 1 → 3<br>less → more | **2** |
| **TIMING** $T$<br>later events = better outcome | 1 = 2010-2015<br>2 = 2005-2010<br>3 = 2000-2005<br>4 = 1996-2000 | **4** |
| **OPPOSITION** $Op$<br>change resistors vs. advocates | 2 → -2<br>much → much<br>opposition support | **-2** |
| **POWER FACTOR** $P$<br>more individual effect = stronger impact | 1 → 4<br>less → more | **2** |
| **IMPACT INDEX** $I_{AI}$<br>sum of impact factors | 1 → 24<br>low → high | **13** |
| **FORESIGHT FACTOR**<br>levels of foresight available | A → F<br>many → few<br>sources sources | **D** |
| **QUALITY**<br>net effect of Wild Card | + positive<br>- negative<br>± both | **–** |

**FORESIGHT SOURCES**

# AN ILLITERATE, DYSFUNCTIONAL NEW GENERATION

Shortcomings in the urban public school systems come home to roost. In a short period of time it is discovered that a large number of graduates cannot cope effectively in the info-technology marketplace—society has no meaningful work for them. These young people have not been trained to understand the dynamics of a highly interdependent, rapidly changing society. Their response is to fight the system that they fear.

## POSSIBLE IMPLICATIONS

### VALUES

Might create an "anti-technology" backlash.

### LEARNING

Massive revitalization of the educational system; dissatisfied parents take matters into their own hands, the growth of home and private schools proliferates.

### GROUP RELATIONSHIPS

Increasing disparity between the haves and have-nots would ripen the possibilities of cultural conflict; as social problems increased, so would the pressures on the government to remedy the situation.

- Large scale failure of school districts is creating great problems in both urban and inner city areas.

- Unwillingness of unions and other players of educational system to adapt to contemporary demands.

## FORESIGHT SOURCES

| IMPACT FACTORS | CHANGE SCALE | |
|---|---|---|
| **RATE OF CHANGE** ΔC<br>faster change = more impact | 1 = years<br>2 = months<br>3 = days | **1** |
| **REACH** R<br>wider reach = more impact | 1 → 5<br>local → global | **2** |
| **VULNERABILITY** V<br>less adaptable = more vulnerable | 1 → 3<br>less → more | **3** |
| **OUTCOME** O<br>more uncertainty = more impact | 1 → 3<br>less → more | **3** |
| **TIMING** T<br>later events = better outcome | 1 = 2010-2015<br>2 = 2005-2010<br>3 = 2000-2005<br>4 = 1996-2000 | **2** |
| **OPPOSITION** Op<br>change resistors vs. advocates | 2 → -2<br>much → much<br>opposition support | **-2** |
| **POWER FACTOR** P<br>more individual effect = stronger impact | 1 → 4<br>less → more | **2** |
| **IMPACT INDEX** I_AI<br>sum of impact factors | 1 → 24<br>low → high | **11** |
| **FORESIGHT FACTOR**<br>levels of foresight available | A → F<br>many → few<br>sources sources | **A** |
| **QUALITY**<br>net effect of Wild Card | + positive<br>- negative<br>± both | **–** |

# NANOTECHNOLOGY TAKES OFF

Nanotechnology – the process of using molecular-sized machines to build useable human-scale products by stacking individual atoms into predetermined configurations – produces usable products. Traditional industrial methods of manufacturing become obsolete. Manufacturing dilemmas that once appeared unsolvable, suddenly become trivial in the face of molecular-level solutions.

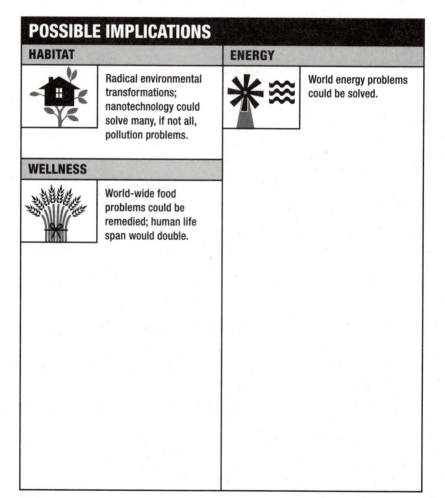

## POSSIBLE IMPLICATIONS

### HABITAT
Radical environmental transformations; nanotechnology could solve many, if not all, pollution problems.

### ENERGY
World energy problems could be solved.

### WELLNESS
World-wide food problems could be remedied; human life span would double.

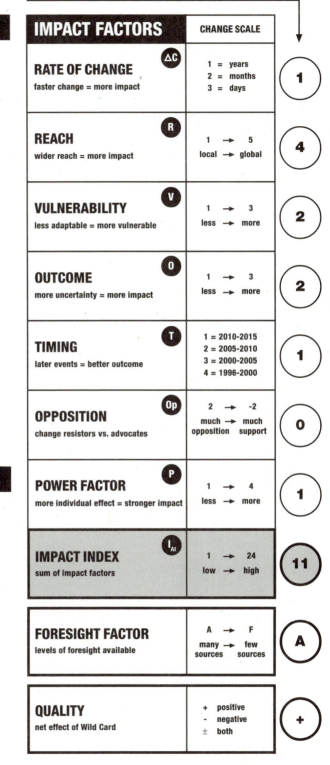

### EARLY INDICATORS

- Growing international research effort in the area.
- College programs/degrees on the subject (1995).

### FORESIGHT SOURCES

- *The Foresight Institute*

| IMPACT FACTORS | CHANGE SCALE | |
|---|---|---|
| **RATE OF CHANGE** $\Delta c$ <br> faster change = more impact | 1 = years <br> 2 = months <br> 3 = days | 1 |
| **REACH** R <br> wider reach = more impact | 1 → 5 <br> local → global | 4 |
| **VULNERABILITY** V <br> less adaptable = more vulnerable | 1 → 3 <br> less → more | 2 |
| **OUTCOME** O <br> more uncertainty = more impact | 1 → 3 <br> less → more | 2 |
| **TIMING** T <br> later events = better outcome | 1 = 2010-2015 <br> 2 = 2005-2010 <br> 3 = 2000-2005 <br> 4 = 1996-2000 | 1 |
| **OPPOSITION** Op <br> change resistors vs. advocates | 2 → -2 <br> much → much <br> opposition support | 0 |
| **POWER FACTOR** P <br> more individual effect = stronger impact | 1 → 4 <br> less → more | 1 |
| **IMPACT INDEX** $I_{AI}$ <br> sum of impact factors | 1 → 24 <br> low → high | 11 |
| **FORESIGHT FACTOR** <br> levels of foresight available | A → F <br> many → few <br> sources sources | A |
| **QUALITY** <br> net effect of Wild Card | + positive <br> - negative <br> ± both | + |

# STOCK MARKET CRASH

The global financial markets collapse suddenly, in response to a surprise negative event, (such as a report that the Ebola virus appears to be out of control,) which punctuates a period of decreasing public confidence in the system. Panic spreads, and within a short period of time almost two-thirds of peak value has been lost.

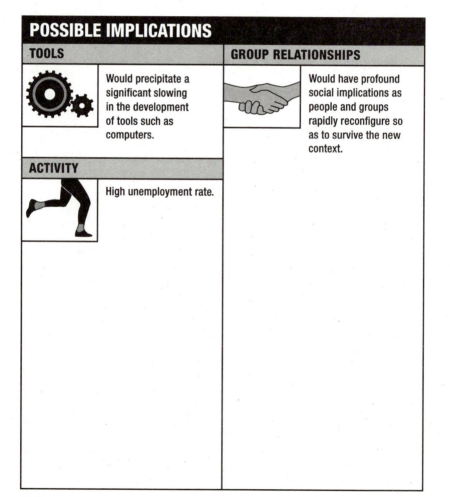

## POSSIBLE IMPLICATIONS

### TOOLS

Would precipitate a significant slowing in the development of tools such as computers.

### ACTIVITY

High unemployment rate.

### GROUP RELATIONSHIPS

Would have profound social implications as people and groups rapidly reconfigure so as to survive the new context.

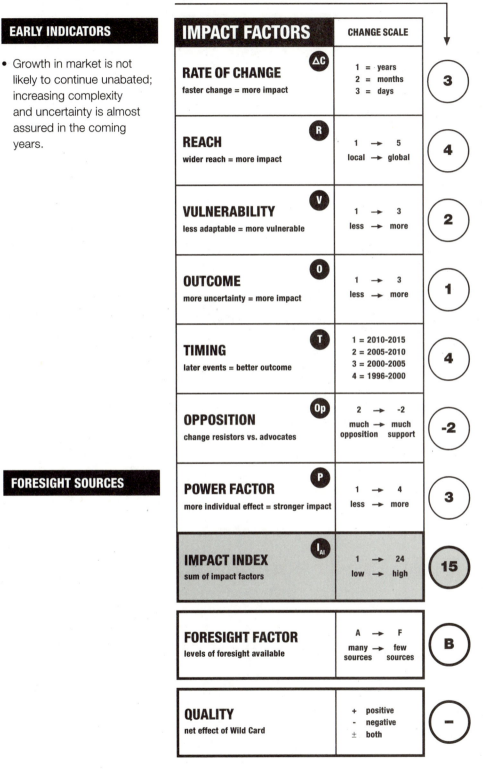

### EARLY INDICATORS

- Growth in market is not likely to continue unabated; increasing complexity and uncertainty is almost assured in the coming years.

### FORESIGHT SOURCES

**IMPACT FACTORS** | **CHANGE SCALE**

**RATE OF CHANGE** (ΔC)
faster change = more impact
- 1 = years
- 2 = months
- 3 = days
→ **3**

**REACH** (R)
wider reach = more impact
1 → 5
local → global
→ **4**

**VULNERABILITY** (V)
less adaptable = more vulnerable
1 → 3
less → more
→ **2**

**OUTCOME** (O)
more uncertainty = more impact
1 → 3
less → more
→ **1**

**TIMING** (T)
later events = better outcome
- 1 = 2010-2015
- 2 = 2005-2010
- 3 = 2000-2005
- 4 = 1996-2000
→ **4**

**OPPOSITION** (Op)
change resistors vs. advocates
2 → -2
much opposition → much support
→ **-2**

**POWER FACTOR** (P)
more individual effect = stronger impact
1 → 4
less → more
→ **3**

**IMPACT INDEX** (I_AI)
sum of impact factors
1 → 24
low → high
→ **15**

**FORESIGHT FACTOR**
levels of foresight available
A → F
many sources → few sources
→ **B**

**QUALITY**
net effect of Wild Card
- + positive
- - negative
- ± both
→ **–**

# HACKERS BLACKMAIL THE FEDERAL RESERVE

An outside source proves to the U.S. Federal Reserve (or the New York Stock Exchange) that their computers can be both manipulated and immobilized at will. Blackmailers demand billions of dollars or they will crash the entire system.

## POSSIBLE IMPLICATIONS

| VALUES | GROUP RELATIONSHIPS |
|---|---|
| Tremendous loss of faith in financial system. | Public loses confidence in the government to control such situations. |

# WILD CARD EQUATION

## EARLY INDICATORS

- Our increasing dependency upon info systems, puts us in an increasingly vulnerable position.

## FORESIGHT SOURCES

- *Winn Schwartau, National Computer Security Association*

| IMPACT FACTORS | CHANGE SCALE | |
|---|---|---|
| **RATE OF CHANGE** ΔC<br>faster change = more impact | 1 = years<br>2 = months<br>3 = days | **3** |
| **REACH** R<br>wider reach = more impact | 1 → 5<br>local → global | **4** |
| **VULNERABILITY** V<br>less adaptable = more vulnerable | 1 → 3<br>less → more | **2** |
| **OUTCOME** O<br>more uncertainty = more impact | 1 → 3<br>less → more | **2** |
| **TIMING** T<br>later events = better outcome | 1 = 2010-2015<br>2 = 2005-2010<br>3 = 2000-2005<br>4 = 1996-2000 | **3** |
| **OPPOSITION** Op<br>change resistors vs. advocates | 2 → -2<br>much → much<br>opposition support | **-2** |
| **POWER FACTOR** P<br>more individual effect = stronger impact | 1 → 4<br>less → more | **2** |
| **IMPACT INDEX** I$_{AI}$<br>sum of impact factors | 1 → 24<br>low → high | **14** |
| **FORESIGHT FACTOR**<br>levels of foresight available | A → F<br>many → few<br>sources sources | **B** |
| **QUALITY**<br>net effect of Wild Card | + positive<br>- negative<br>± both | **–** |

# GLOBAL FINANCIAL REVOLUTION - E-CASH IS THE REIGNING COMMERCE

The Internet leads to the end of money as we know it, possibly along with taxation. All cash transactions are effectively eliminated in a short period of time, via the instantaneous monetary transactions taking place electronically—and for the most part, anonymously, thanks to encryption. The elimination of cash transactions clears the stage for a variety of criminal acts.

## POSSIBLE IMPLICATIONS

| ACTIVITY | TOOLS |
|---|---|
|  Federal and state income tax shrinks, governmental panic; dash toward Internet and information technology. |  Would create a tremendous dependency upon computers and computer networks. |

## EARLY INDICATORS

- Move toward smart cards, it is forecasted that by 2010, there will be a billion smart cards in use in America.
- Rapid development of the Internet and World Wide Web.
- Many "e-cash" companies.
- Free encryption available.

## FORESIGHT SOURCES

- *Wired Magazine*
- *Upside Magazine*

| IMPACT FACTORS | CHANGE SCALE | |
|---|---|---|
| **RATE OF CHANGE** $\Delta C$<br>faster change = more impact | 1 = years<br>2 = months<br>3 = days | **1** |
| **REACH** $R$<br>wider reach = more impact | 1 → 5<br>local → global | **5** |
| **VULNERABILITY** $V$<br>less adaptable = more vulnerable | 1 → 3<br>less → more | **2** |
| **OUTCOME** $O$<br>more uncertainty = more impact | 1 → 3<br>less → more | **2** |
| **TIMING** $T$<br>later events = better outcome | 1 = 2010-2015<br>2 = 2005-2010<br>3 = 2000-2005<br>4 = 1996-2000 | **2** |
| **OPPOSITION** $Op$<br>change resistors vs. advocates | 2 → -2<br>much → much<br>opposition support | **-2** |
| **POWER FACTOR** $P$<br>more individual effect = stronger impact | 1 → 4<br>less → more | **3** |
| **IMPACT INDEX** $I_{AI}$<br>sum of impact factors | 1 → 24<br>low → high | **13** |
| **FORESIGHT FACTOR**<br>levels of foresight available | A → F<br>many → few<br>sources sources | **A** |
| **QUALITY**<br>net effect of Wild Card | + positive<br>- negative<br>± both | **+** |

131

# "SECOND" WORLD NATION DEMONSTRATES NANOTECH WEAPONS

In a major surprise to the West, a second world nation convincingly demonstrates a molecular-sized machine which can be programmed to disable any of a number of conventional weapons systems and attack humans on demand.

## POSSIBLE IMPLICATIONS

| TOOLS | GROUP RELATIONSHIPS |
|---|---|
|  All conventional weapons systems could be rendered directly vulnerable. |  Could stir great insecurity in the West; potential for global blackmail; reorganization of world geopolitics; there would be fear since the machines are invisible. |

# WILD CARD EQUATION

- More work being done on nanotech outside of U.S. than within; major power fixation on variations of present force structure.

| IMPACT FACTORS | | CHANGE SCALE | |
|---|---|---|---|
| **RATE OF CHANGE** (ΔC)<br>faster change = more impact | | 1 = years<br>2 = months<br>3 = days | **2** |
| **REACH** (R)<br>wider reach = more impact | | 1 → 5<br>local → global | **4** |
| **VULNERABILITY** (V)<br>less adaptable = more vulnerable | | 1 → 3<br>less → more | **2** |
| **OUTCOME** (O)<br>more uncertainty = more impact | | 1 → 3<br>less → more | **3** |
| **TIMING** (T)<br>later events = better outcome | | 1 = 2010-2015<br>2 = 2005-2010<br>3 = 2000-2005<br>4 = 1996-2000 | **1** |
| **OPPOSITION** (Op)<br>change resistors vs. advocates | | 2 → -2<br>much → much<br>opposition support | **0** |
| **POWER FACTOR** (P)<br>more individual effect = stronger impact | | 1 → 4<br>less → more | **2** |
| **IMPACT INDEX** ($I_{AI}$)<br>sum of impact factors | | 1 → 24<br>low → high | **14** |
| **FORESIGHT FACTOR**<br>levels of foresight available | | A → F<br>many → few<br>sources sources | **B** |
| **QUALITY**<br>net effect of Wild Card | | + positive<br>- negative<br>± both | **±** |

## FORESIGHT SOURCES

- *The Foresight Institute*

# HUMANS DIRECTLY INTERFACE WITH THE NET

A subderminally implanted computer chip, or another transducing device, allows instantaneous, two-way thought-based access to the Web. Through specially designed contact lenses or glasses, a direct display of the retrieved information is superimposed on one's field of view. Vast global networks are accessible from any location, at all times, including databases and programs, as well as other individuals.

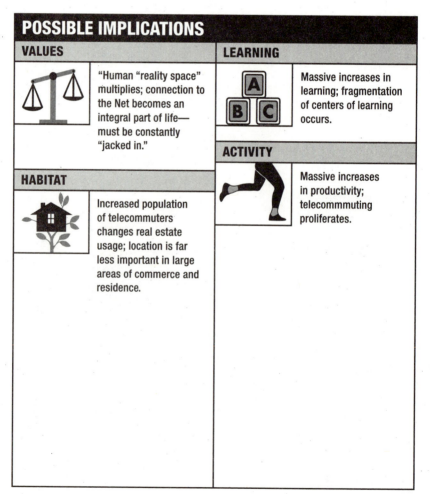

## POSSIBLE IMPLICATIONS

### VALUES

"Human "reality space" multiplies; connection to the Net becomes an integral part of life—must be constantly "jacked in."

### LEARNING

Massive increases in learning; fragmentation of centers of learning occurs.

### ACTIVITY

Massive increases in productivity; telecommmuting proliferates.

### HABITAT

Increased population of telecommuters changes real estate usage; location is far less important in large areas of commerce and residence.

## EARLY INDICATORS

- Great strides in understanding operation of brain.
- Development of nerve chips in which electronics directly interface with nerves.
- Advances in display and observational technology that are increasingly linked closely to the human eye.
- Simple computer games controlled by human thoughts on the market in 1995.

## FORESIGHT SOURCES

- *MIT Media Lab*
- *Brain research*
- *New computer games*

| IMPACT FACTORS | CHANGE SCALE | |
|---|---|---|
| **RATE OF CHANGE** △c<br>faster change = more impact | 1 = years<br>2 = months<br>3 = days | **1** |
| **REACH** R<br>wider reach = more impact | 1 → 5<br>local → global | **4** |
| **VULNERABILITY** V<br>less adaptable = more vulnerable | 1 → 3<br>less → more | **1** |
| **OUTCOME** O<br>more uncertainty = more impact | 1 → 3<br>less → more | **1** |
| **TIMING** T<br>later events = better outcome | 1 = 2010-2015<br>2 = 2005-2010<br>3 = 2000-2005<br>4 = 1996-2000 | **1** |
| **OPPOSITION** Op<br>change resistors vs. advocates | 2 → -2<br>much → much<br>opposition → support | **-2** |
| **POWER FACTOR** P<br>more individual effect = stronger impact | 1 → 4<br>less → more | **5** |
| **IMPACT INDEX** $I_{AI}$<br>sum of impact factors | 1 → 24<br>low → high | **11** |
| **FORESIGHT FACTOR**<br>levels of foresight available | A → F<br>many → few<br>sources sources | **A** |
| **QUALITY**<br>net effect of Wild Card | + positive<br>- negative<br>± both | **+** |

# ENCRYPTION INVALIDATED

A computing breakthrough makes it possible to crack almost any traditional encryption code with generally available hardware.

## POSSIBLE IMPLICATIONS

### COMMUNICATION

New measures would be developed to safeguard corporate, personal and government information.

### TOOLS

International scramble to manufacture a new, superior encryption product.

### GROUP RELATIONSHIPS

Radical rethinking of day-to-day operation and philosophy of government and commerce.

## WILD CARD EQUATION

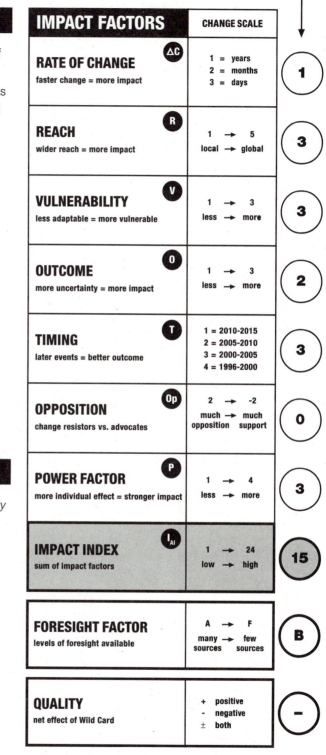

**EARLY INDICATORS**

- Widespread invalidation of digital encryption results.
- Rapid advances in all areas of computing are breaking other constraints.

**FORESIGHT SOURCES**

- *National Computer Security Association*

| IMPACT FACTORS | CHANGE SCALE | |
|---|---|---|
| **RATE OF CHANGE** (ΔC)<br>faster change = more impact | 1 = years<br>2 = months<br>3 = days | 1 |
| **REACH** (R)<br>wider reach = more impact | 1 → 5<br>local → global | 3 |
| **VULNERABILITY** (V)<br>less adaptable = more vulnerable | 1 → 3<br>less → more | 3 |
| **OUTCOME** (O)<br>more uncertainty = more impact | 1 → 3<br>less → more | 2 |
| **TIMING** (T)<br>later events = better outcome | 1 = 2010-2015<br>2 = 2005-2010<br>3 = 2000-2005<br>4 = 1996-2000 | 3 |
| **OPPOSITION** (Op)<br>change resistors vs. advocates | 2 → -2<br>much → much<br>opposition support | 0 |
| **POWER FACTOR** (P)<br>more individual effect = stronger impact | 1 → 4<br>less → more | 3 |
| **IMPACT INDEX** (I_AI)<br>sum of impact factors | 1 → 24<br>low → high | 15 |
| **FORESIGHT FACTOR**<br>levels of foresight available | A → F<br>many → few<br>sources sources | B |
| **QUALITY**<br>net effect of Wild Card | + positive<br>- negative<br>± both | – |

# VIRTUAL REALITY AND HOLOGRAPHY MOVE INFORMATION, INSTEAD OF PEOPLE

The Internet, advances in Virtual Reality, and projection holography make it possible to effectively carry out business from wherever one can access the Net—anywhere on earth. The imagery fidelity is such that the electronic interface sufficiently mimics human-to-human interface. Individuals can present whatever persona they desire.

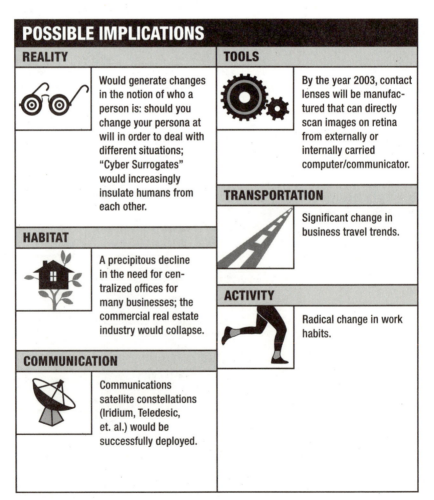

## POSSIBLE IMPLICATIONS

### REALITY

Would generate changes in the notion of who a person is: should you change your persona at will in order to deal with different situations; "Cyber Surrogates" would increasingly insulate humans from each other.

### HABITAT

A precipitous decline in the need for centralized offices for many businesses; the commercial real estate industry would collapse.

### COMMUNICATION

Communications satellite constellations (Iridium, Teledesic, et. al.) would be successfully deployed.

### TOOLS

By the year 2003, contact lenses will be manufactured that can directly scan images on retina from externally or internally carried computer/communicator.

### TRANSPORTATION

Significant change in business travel trends.

### ACTIVITY

Radical change in work habits.

# WILD CARD EQUATION

## EARLY INDICATORS

- Advances in groupware.
- Similar trends in many other areas: remotely accessed military sensor systems, multimedia on web, telephone on the Net.
- Advances in computer thought recognition.

## FORESIGHT SOURCES

- *VR magazines*
- *Media lab at MIT*
- *Groupware start-ups*

| IMPACT FACTORS | CHANGE SCALE | |
|---|---|---|
| **RATE OF CHANGE** ΔC<br>faster change = more impact | 1 = years<br>2 = months<br>3 = days | **1** |
| **REACH** R<br>wider reach = more impact | 1 → 5<br>local → global | **3** |
| **VULNERABILITY** V<br>less adaptable = more vulnerable | 1 → 3<br>less → more | **2** |
| **OUTCOME** O<br>more uncertainty = more impact | 1 → 3<br>less → more | **1** |
| **TIMING** T<br>later events = better outcome | 1 = 2010-2015<br>2 = 2005-2010<br>3 = 2000-2005<br>4 = 1996-2000 | **2** |
| **OPPOSITION** Op<br>change resistors vs. advocates | 2 → -2<br>much → much<br>opposition → support | **0** |
| **POWER FACTOR** P<br>more individual effect = stronger impact | 1 → 4<br>less → more | **3** |
| **IMPACT INDEX** $I_{AI}$<br>sum of impact factors | 1 → 24<br>low → high | **12** |
| **FORESIGHT FACTOR**<br>levels of foresight available | A → F<br>many → few<br>sources → sources | **A** |
| **QUALITY**<br>net effect of Wild Card | + positive<br>- negative<br>± both | **+** |

# FASTER THAN LIGHT SPEED TRAVEL

Beam me up...Scientists discover how to "engineer space/time" and in so doing, reduce mass to zero within a given volume, can then instantaneously transfer the contents of the "craft" to another location.

## POSSIBLE IMPLICATIONS

### REALITY

Faster than light travel would establish the possibility of extraterrestrial life, it would no longer be impossible to visit or be visited from a far distance galaxy; it would raise the possibility of time travel.

### GROUP RELATIONSHIPS

Would revolutionize militaries allowing rapid movement of forces, even at fractions of the Speed of Light; proprietary rights issues would inflame tension and/or unity amongst countries on earth.

### TRANSPORTATION

Space exploration possibilities would explode, as would terrestrial applications.

# WILD CARD EQUATION

## EARLY INDICATORS

- Serious scientists, including those of the United States Air Force, are currently experimenting to identify the engineering problems associated with this faster than light speed travel. Experts contend that there is a good chance that a breakthrough in this area may occur in the next decade.

- Mathematics proves that this it is now theoretically possible.

- Experiments in 1995 show a particle moving at 7.2 times the speed of light.

## FORESIGHT SOURCES

- *United States Air Force*
- *Web Sites*
- *Society for Scientific Exploration*

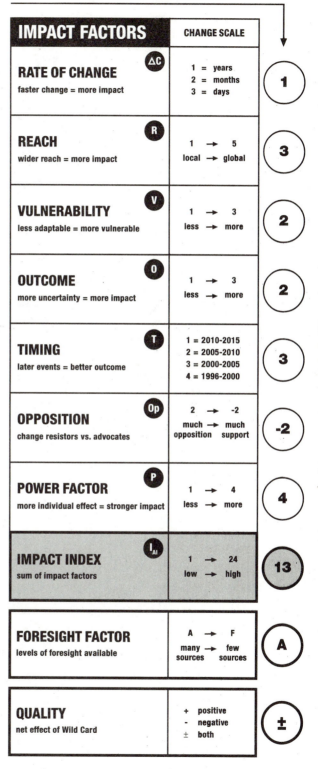

| IMPACT FACTORS | CHANGE SCALE | |
|---|---|---|
| **RATE OF CHANGE** $\Delta c$<br>faster change = more impact | 1 = years<br>2 = months<br>3 = days | **1** |
| **REACH** $R$<br>wider reach = more impact | 1 → 5<br>local → global | **3** |
| **VULNERABILITY** $V$<br>less adaptable = more vulnerable | 1 → 3<br>less → more | **2** |
| **OUTCOME** $O$<br>more uncertainty = more impact | 1 → 3<br>less → more | **2** |
| **TIMING** $T$<br>later events = better outcome | 1 = 2010-2015<br>2 = 2005-2010<br>3 = 2000-2005<br>4 = 1996-2000 | **3** |
| **OPPOSITION** $Op$<br>change resistors vs. advocates | 2 → -2<br>much → much<br>opposition support | **-2** |
| **POWER FACTOR** $P$<br>more individual effect = stronger impact | 1 → 4<br>less → more | **4** |
| **IMPACT INDEX** $I_{AI}$<br>sum of impact factors | 1 → 24<br>low → high | **13** |
| **FORESIGHT FACTOR**<br>levels of foresight available | A → F<br>many → few<br>sources sources | **A** |
| **QUALITY**<br>net effect of Wild Card | + positive<br>- negative<br>± both | **±** |

# ENERGY REVOLUTION

A scientific breakthrough propels an energy revolution, rendering all of our traditional energy sources, including fossil fuels, obsolete. Cold Fusion and Zero-Point Energy – commercial generators that require no "fuel" in order to produce heat and electricity – become a reality.

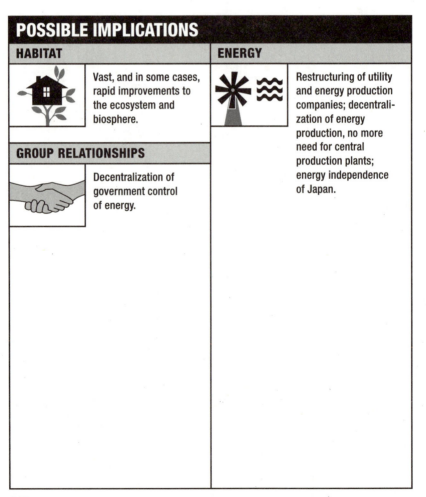

## POSSIBLE IMPLICATIONS

### HABITAT

Vast, and in some cases, rapid improvements to the ecosystem and biosphere.

### GROUP RELATIONSHIPS

Decentralization of government control of energy.

### ENERGY

Restructuring of utility and energy production companies; decentralization of energy production, no more need for central production plants; energy independence of Japan.

- Functioning cold fusion generator reported, (Patterson cell, 1995) with apparent subsequent investment by major U.S. corporation.

- Pattern of broadly-based experiments that sporadically produce over-unity energy.

- *Infinite Energy Magazine*
- *Internet newsgroups (Keely Net)*
- *Society for Scientific Exploration*

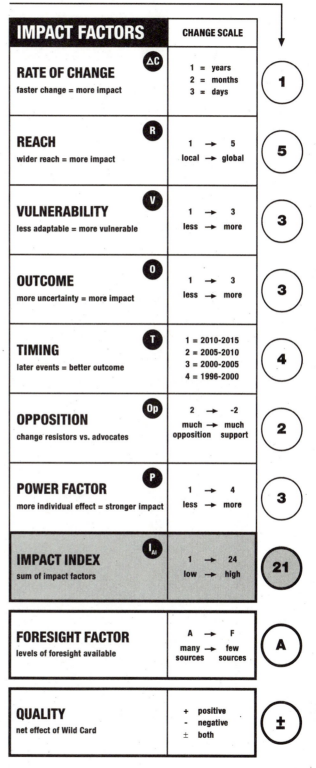

| IMPACT FACTORS | CHANGE SCALE | |
|---|---|---|
| **RATE OF CHANGE** $\Delta c$ <br> faster change = more impact | 1 = years <br> 2 = months <br> 3 = days | **1** |
| **REACH** R <br> wider reach = more impact | 1 → 5 <br> local → global | **5** |
| **VULNERABILITY** V <br> less adaptable = more vulnerable | 1 → 3 <br> less → more | **3** |
| **OUTCOME** O <br> more uncertainty = more impact | 1 → 3 <br> less → more | **3** |
| **TIMING** T <br> later events = better outcome | 1 = 2010-2015 <br> 2 = 2005-2010 <br> 3 = 2000-2005 <br> 4 = 1996-2000 | **4** |
| **OPPOSITION** Op <br> change resistors vs. advocates | 2 → -2 <br> much → much <br> opposition support | **2** |
| **POWER FACTOR** P <br> more individual effect = stronger impact | 1 → 4 <br> less → more | **3** |
| **IMPACT INDEX** $I_{AI}$ <br> sum of impact factors | 1 → 24 <br> low → high | **21** |
| **FORESIGHT FACTOR** <br> levels of foresight available | A → F <br> many → few <br> sources sources | **A** |
| **QUALITY** <br> net effect of Wild Card | + positive <br> - negative <br> ± both | **±** |

# MASSIVE, LENGTHY DISRUPTION OF NATIONAL ELECTRICAL SUPPLY

A combination of events (weather, terrorism, software errors, etc.) conspire to cause the electrical grid of the U.S. (or a major part of it,) to crash. Important pieces of equipment are destroyed that are not quickly replaceable. Some major components take a up to a year to remanufacture.

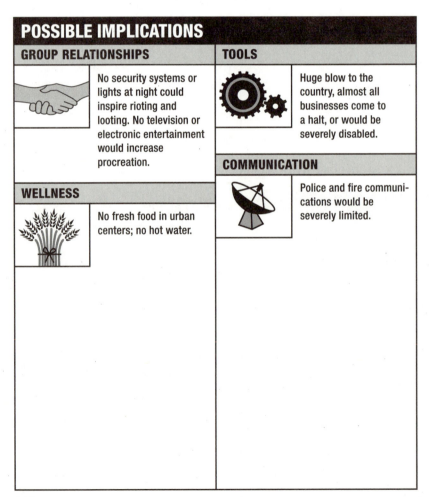

## POSSIBLE IMPLICATIONS

### GROUP RELATIONSHIPS

No security systems or lights at night could inspire rioting and looting. No television or electronic entertainment would increase procreation.

### WELLNESS

No fresh food in urban centers; no hot water.

### TOOLS

Huge blow to the country, almost all businesses come to a halt, or would be severely disabled.

### COMMUNICATION

Police and fire communications would be severely limited.

## EARLY INDICATORS

- Crash of western U.S. grid in June 1996.
- Increasing complexity (and vulnerability) of computer code and control systems.
- Physical vulnerability of key nodes of system.

## FORESIGHT SOURCES

- *Power companies*
- *Federal Emergency Management Agency*
- *Industry associations*

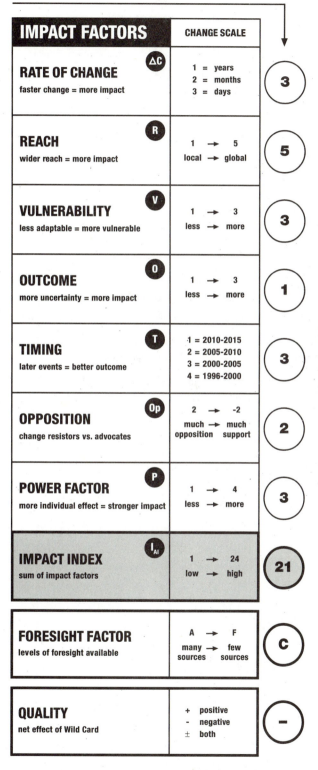

| IMPACT FACTORS | CHANGE SCALE | |
|---|---|---|
| **RATE OF CHANGE** $\Delta c$ <br> faster change = more impact | 1 = years <br> 2 = months <br> 3 = days | **3** |
| **REACH** $R$ <br> wider reach = more impact | 1 → 5 <br> local → global | **5** |
| **VULNERABILITY** $V$ <br> less adaptable = more vulnerable | 1 → 3 <br> less → more | **3** |
| **OUTCOME** $O$ <br> more uncertainty = more impact | 1 → 3 <br> less → more | **1** |
| **TIMING** $T$ <br> later events = better outcome | 1 = 2010-2015 <br> 2 = 2005-2010 <br> 3 = 2000-2005 <br> 4 = 1996-2000 | **3** |
| **OPPOSITION** $Op$ <br> change resistors vs. advocates | 2 → -2 <br> much → much <br> opposition support | **2** |
| **POWER FACTOR** $P$ <br> more individual effect = stronger impact | 1 → 4 <br> less → more | **3** |
| **IMPACT INDEX** $I_{AI}$ <br> sum of impact factors | 1 → 24 <br> low → high | **21** |
| **FORESIGHT FACTOR** <br> levels of foresight available | A → F <br> many → few <br> sources sources | **C** |
| **QUALITY** <br> net effect of Wild Card | + positive <br> - negative <br> ± both | **–** |

# ROOM TEMPERATURE SUPERCONDUCTIVITY ARRIVES

New discoveries invent easily manufacturable wires and other conductors that are superconductive at room temperature. Motors and other electrical devices can be built one-quarter of the previous size and long-term electrical requirements could decrease by seventy percent.

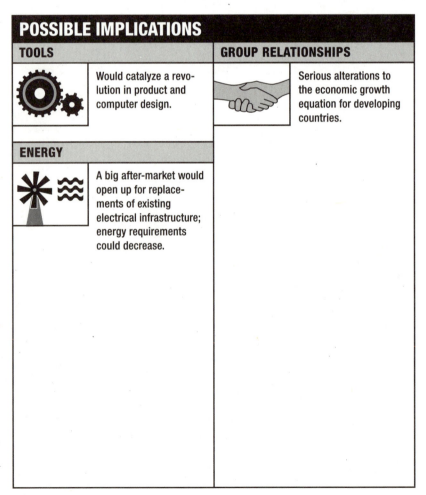

## POSSIBLE IMPLICATIONS

### TOOLS

Would catalyze a revolution in product and computer design.

### ENERGY

A big after-market would open up for replacements of existing electrical infrastructure; energy requirements could decrease.

### GROUP RELATIONSHIPS

Serious alterations to the economic growth equation for developing countries.

**EARLY INDICATORS**

- Continued advancements in superconductivity research.
- Major changes in electric industry at all levels.

**FORESIGHT SOURCES**

| IMPACT FACTORS | CHANGE SCALE | |
|---|---|---|
| **RATE OF CHANGE** ΔC<br>faster change = more impact | 1 = years<br>2 = months<br>3 = days | **1** |
| **REACH** R<br>wider reach = more impact | 1 → 5<br>local → global | **4** |
| **VULNERABILITY** V<br>less adaptable = more vulnerable | 1 → 3<br>less → more | **1** |
| **OUTCOME** O<br>more uncertainty = more impact | 1 → 3<br>less → more | **1** |
| **TIMING** T<br>later events = better outcome | 1 = 2010-2015<br>2 = 2005-2010<br>3 = 2000-2005<br>4 = 1996-2000 | **2** |
| **OPPOSITION** Op<br>change resistors vs. advocates | 2 → -2<br>much → much<br>opposition support | **2** |
| **POWER FACTOR** P<br>more individual effect = stronger impact | 1 → 4<br>less → more | **1** |
| **IMPACT INDEX** I$_{AI}$<br>sum of impact factors | 1 → 24<br>low → high | **14** |
| **FORESIGHT FACTOR**<br>levels of foresight available | A → F<br>many → few<br>sources sources | **B** |
| **QUALITY**<br>net effect of Wild Card | + positive<br>- negative<br>± both | **+** |

# FUEL CELLS REPLACE INTERNAL COMBUSTION ENGINES

Fuel cells that provide cheap, clean power (either from hydrogen-based supply or from existing liquid fossil fuels,) quickly become the principal source for surface and ocean transportation.

## POSSIBLE IMPLICATIONS

### HABITAT

Significant decrease in atmospheric pollution; potentially the greenhouse effect would be reversed.

### ENERGY

The global energy infrastructure would be reformed.

### ACTIVITY

New business opportunities would explode.

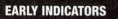

### EARLY INDICATORS

- Legislation to produce pollution-free cars in California and New England by the end of decade.
- Significant breakthroughs in fuel cell technology.

### FORESIGHT SOURCES

- *Ballard Company*
- *Ford Motor Company*
- *Directed Technologies Inc.*
- *The Rocky Mountain Institute*

## IMPACT FACTORS

| IMPACT FACTORS | CHANGE SCALE | |
|---|---|---|
| **RATE OF CHANGE** $\Delta c$ <br> faster change = more impact | 1 = years <br> 2 = months <br> 3 = days | **1** |
| **REACH** $R$ <br> wider reach = more impact | 1 → 5 <br> local → global | **3** |
| **VULNERABILITY** $V$ <br> less adaptable = more vulnerable | 1 → 3 <br> less → more | **1** |
| **OUTCOME** $O$ <br> more uncertainty = more impact | 1 → 3 <br> less → more | **1** |
| **TIMING** $T$ <br> later events = better outcome | 1 = 2010-2015 <br> 2 = 2005-2010 <br> 3 = 2000-2005 <br> 4 = 1996-2000 | **3** |
| **OPPOSITION** $Op$ <br> change resistors vs. advocates | 2 → -2 <br> much → much <br> opposition support | **2** |
| **POWER FACTOR** $P$ <br> more individual effect = stronger impact | 1 → 4 <br> less → more | **2** |
| **IMPACT INDEX** $I_{AI}$ <br> sum of impact factors | 1 → 24 <br> low → high | **14** |
| **FORESIGHT FACTOR** <br> levels of foresight available | A → F <br> many → few <br> sources sources | **B** |
| **QUALITY** <br> net effect of Wild Card | + positive <br> - negative <br> ± both | **+** |

# COLD FUSION IS EMBRACED BY A DEVELOPING COUNTRY

A developing country such as China, India, or Pakistan leaps into contention with the West by embracing cold fusion technology, which produces electricity so cheaply it is virtually free. That country greatly expands its electrical power base in places that do not yet have well-established infrastructure and begins building "free-energy" generators.

## POSSIBLE IMPLICATIONS

### GROUP RELATIONSHIPS

Enables extraordinarily rapid economic development; the technology may be utilized by the military for less-than-altruistic purposes.

# WILD CARD EQUATION

## EARLY INDICATORS

- Apparent breakthrough in U.S. and Japan, great interest in technology by countries like India.

## FORESIGHT SOURCES

- *Infinite Energy Magazine*
- *Cold Fusion Magazine*
- *Internet newsgroup*

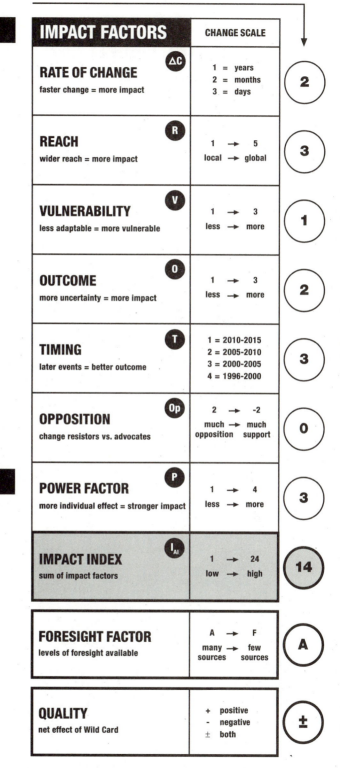

| IMPACT FACTORS | CHANGE SCALE | |
|---|---|---|
| **RATE OF CHANGE** $\Delta c$<br>faster change = more impact | 1 = years<br>2 = months<br>3 = days | **2** |
| **REACH** R<br>wider reach = more impact | 1 → 5<br>local → global | **3** |
| **VULNERABILITY** V<br>less adaptable = more vulnerable | 1 → 3<br>less → more | **1** |
| **OUTCOME** O<br>more uncertainty = more impact | 1 → 3<br>less → more | **2** |
| **TIMING** T<br>later events = better outcome | 1 = 2010-2015<br>2 = 2005-2010<br>3 = 2000-2005<br>4 = 1996-2000 | **3** |
| **OPPOSITION** Op<br>change resistors vs. advocates | 2 → -2<br>much → much<br>opposition support | **0** |
| **POWER FACTOR** P<br>more individual effect = stronger impact | 1 → 4<br>less → more | **3** |
| **IMPACT INDEX** $I_{AI}$<br>sum of impact factors | 1 → 24<br>low → high | **14** |
| **FORESIGHT FACTOR**<br>levels of foresight available | A → F<br>many → few<br>sources sources | **A** |
| **QUALITY**<br>net effect of Wild Card | + positive<br>- negative<br>± both | **±** |

# VIRTUAL REALITY REVOLUTIONIZES EDUCATION

Children and young adults increasingly learn by being immersed into a VR-generated learning environment. Learning is experiencing school anywhere... and everywhere. The quality and amount of learning per time invested explodes – a thirteen year education can be earned in seven years. Information technology rich individuals become dramatically more capable and salable than those who are not.

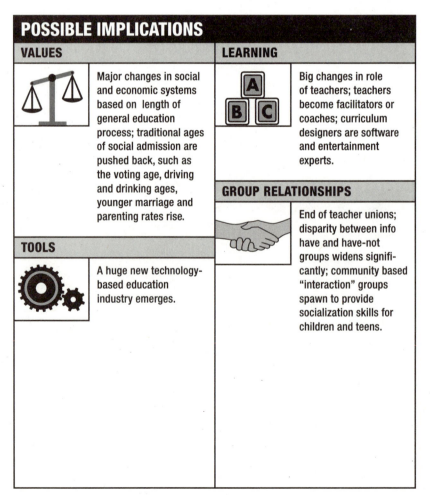

## POSSIBLE IMPLICATIONS

### VALUES

Major changes in social and economic systems based on length of general education process; traditional ages of social admission are pushed back, such as the voting age, driving and drinking ages, younger marriage and parenting rates rise.

### TOOLS

A huge new technology-based education industry emerges.

### LEARNING

Big changes in role of teachers; teachers become facilitators or coaches; curriculum designers are software and entertainment experts.

### GROUP RELATIONSHIPS

End of teacher unions; disparity between info have and have-not groups widens significantly; community based "interaction" groups spawn to provide socialization skills for children and teens.

# WILD CARD EQUATION

## EARLY INDICATORS

- Advances in multimedia have shown dramatic decreases in the time required to learn certain kinds of information. Learning is found to increase by 100%.

- Designs are already in the works for six prototype private schools built around virtual reality to come on line by the turn of the century.

- Over the last decade, The Public Broadcasting Service (PBS) has had a 200% increase in enrollment for distant learning courses.

- Entertainment technology.

## FORESIGHT SOURCES

- *Mind Extension University*
- *Education technology companies*
- *U.S. military*
- *Professor William Halal, George Washington University*

## IMPACT FACTORS

| IMPACT FACTORS | CHANGE SCALE | |
|---|---|---|
| **RATE OF CHANGE** $\Delta c$ <br> faster change = more impact | 1 = years <br> 2 = months <br> 3 = days | **1** |
| **REACH** R <br> wider reach = more impact | 1 → 5 <br> local → global | **4** |
| **VULNERABILITY** V <br> less adaptable = more vulnerable | 1 → 3 <br> less → more | **1** |
| **OUTCOME** O <br> more uncertainty = more impact | 1 → 3 <br> less → more | **1** |
| **TIMING** T <br> later events = better outcome | 1 = 2010-2015 <br> 2 = 2005-2010 <br> 3 = 2000-2005 <br> 4 = 1996-2000 | **0** |
| **OPPOSITION** Op <br> change resistors vs. advocates | 2 → -2 <br> much → much <br> opposition support | **0** |
| **POWER FACTOR** P <br> more individual effect = stronger impact | 1 → 4 <br> less → more | **3** |
| **IMPACT INDEX** $I_{AI}$ <br> sum of impact factors | 1 → 24 <br> low → high | **12** |
| **FORESIGHT FACTOR** <br> levels of foresight available | A → F <br> many → few <br> sources sources | **A** |
| **QUALITY** <br> net effect of Wild Card | + positive <br> - negative <br> ± both | **+** |

# LOSS OF INTELLECTUAL PROPERTY RIGHTS

A rapid series of Supreme Court decisions makes it clear that information cannot be controlled or owned and is neither tangible nor containable. The rights of intellectual property are impossible to effectively identify and constrain. Information becomes a free commodity.

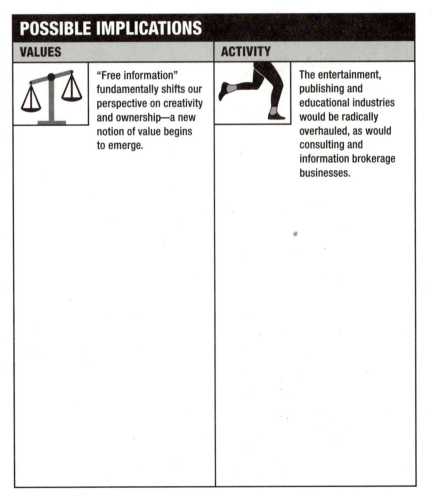

## POSSIBLE IMPLICATIONS

| VALUES | ACTIVITY |
|---|---|
| "Free information" fundamentally shifts our perspective on creativity and ownership—a new notion of value begins to emerge. | The entertainment, publishing and educational industries would be radically overhauled, as would consulting and information brokerage businesses. |

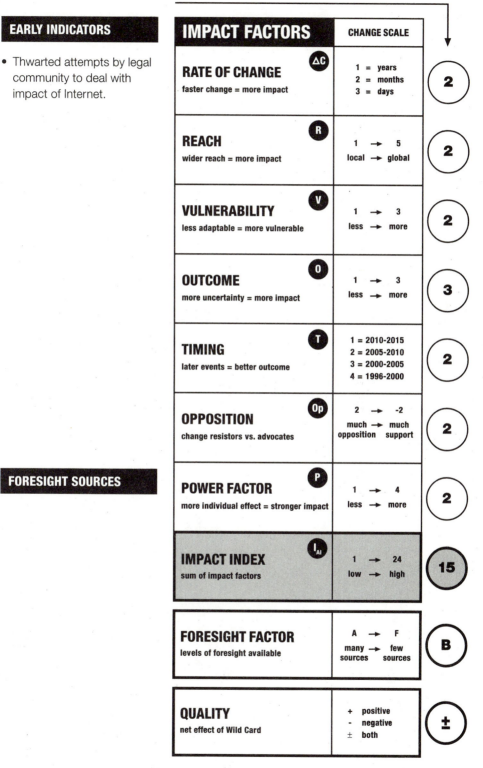

## WILD CARD EQUATION

### EARLY INDICATORS

- Thwarted attempts by legal community to deal with impact of Internet.

### FORESIGHT SOURCES

| IMPACT FACTORS | CHANGE SCALE | |
|---|---|---|
| **RATE OF CHANGE** (ΔC)<br>faster change = more impact | 1 = years<br>2 = months<br>3 = days | **2** |
| **REACH** (R)<br>wider reach = more impact | 1 → 5<br>local → global | **2** |
| **VULNERABILITY** (V)<br>less adaptable = more vulnerable | 1 → 3<br>less → more | **2** |
| **OUTCOME** (O)<br>more uncertainty = more impact | 1 → 3<br>less → more | **3** |
| **TIMING** (T)<br>later events = better outcome | 1 = 2010-2015<br>2 = 2005-2010<br>3 = 2000-2005<br>4 = 1996-2000 | **2** |
| **OPPOSITION** (Op)<br>change resistors vs. advocates | 2 → -2<br>much → much<br>opposition support | **2** |
| **POWER FACTOR** (P)<br>more individual effect = stronger impact | 1 → 4<br>less → more | **2** |
| **IMPACT INDEX** ($I_{AI}$)<br>sum of impact factors | 1 → 24<br>low → high | **15** |
| **FORESIGHT FACTOR**<br>levels of foresight available | A → F<br>many → few<br>sources sources | **B** |
| **QUALITY**<br>net effect of Wild Card | + positive<br>- negative<br>± both | **±** |

# AFRICA UNRAVELS

The combination of increasing population growth and poverty; deadly epidemics, famine, and environmental degradation; with political instability, pushes much of equatorial Africa over the edge. Large-scale rebellions roll across the continent, anarchy is reigning.

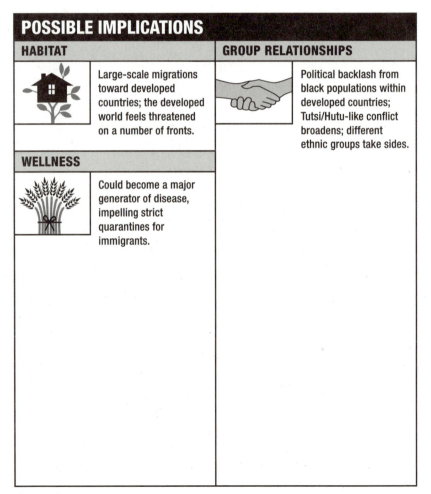

## POSSIBLE IMPLICATIONS

### HABITAT

Large-scale migrations toward developed countries; the developed world feels threatened on a number of fronts.

### WELLNESS

Could become a major generator of disease, impelling strict quarantines for immigrants.

### GROUP RELATIONSHIPS

Political backlash from black populations within developed countries; Tutsi/Hutu-like conflict broadens; different ethnic groups take sides.

# WILD CARD EQUATION

- The potential sources for instability already exist in various combinations throughout the continent. Africa seems to be getting worse, rather than better.

- Pressures (population growth, disease outbreaks) are likely to increase before they abate.

| IMPACT FACTORS | CHANGE SCALE | |
|---|---|---|
| **RATE OF CHANGE** $\Delta c$ <br> faster change = more impact | 1 = years <br> 2 = months <br> 3 = days | 1 |
| **REACH** R <br> wider reach = more impact | 1 → 5 <br> local → global | 2 |
| **VULNERABILITY** V <br> less adaptable = more vulnerable | 1 → 3 <br> less → more | 2 |
| **OUTCOME** O <br> more uncertainty = more impact | 1 → 3 <br> less → more | 3 |
| **TIMING** T <br> later events = better outcome | 1 = 2010-2015 <br> 2 = 2005-2010 <br> 3 = 2000-2005 <br> 4 = 1996-2000 | 3 |
| **OPPOSITION** Op <br> change resistors vs. advocates | 2 → -2 <br> much → much <br> opposition support | 0 |
| **POWER FACTOR** P <br> more individual effect = stronger impact | 1 → 4 <br> less → more | 1 |
| **IMPACT INDEX** $I_{AI}$ <br> sum of impact factors | 1 → 24 <br> low → high | 12 |
| **FORESIGHT FACTOR** <br> levels of foresight available | A → F <br> many → few <br> sources sources | A |
| **QUALITY** <br> net effect of Wild Card | + positive <br> - negative <br> ± both | – |

- *United Nations*
- *Non Government Organizations*

# COLLAPSE OF THE U.S. DOLLAR

The world financial community loses confidence in the abilities of the U.S. government and Federal Reserve to forestall a quickly approaching "day of reckoning" with the federal debt. Global money managers switch to a more stable currency as the index for world trade.

## POSSIBLE IMPLICATIONS

| ACTIVITY | GROUP RELATIONSHIPS |
|---|---|
| Great changes in global money focus, shifts in jobs. | Another country becomes the de facto economic leader of world. |

## WILD CARD EQUATION

### EARLY INDICATORS

- Continued growth of national debt.
- U.S. economy increasingly effected by foreign financial swings.

### FORESIGHT SOURCES

| IMPACT FACTORS | CHANGE SCALE | |
|---|---|---|
| **RATE OF CHANGE** (ΔC)<br>faster change = more impact | 1 = years<br>2 = months<br>3 = days | **2** |
| **REACH** (R)<br>wider reach = more impact | 1 → 5<br>local → global | **3** |
| **VULNERABILITY** (V)<br>less adaptable = more vulnerable | 1 → 3<br>less → more | **1** |
| **OUTCOME** (O)<br>more uncertainty = more impact | 1 → 3<br>less → more | **3** |
| **TIMING** (T)<br>later events = better outcome | 1 = 2010-2015<br>2 = 2005-2010<br>3 = 2000-2005<br>4 = 1996-2000 | **4** |
| **OPPOSITION** (Op)<br>change resistors vs. advocates | 2 → -2<br>much → much<br>opposition support | **1** |
| **POWER FACTOR** (P)<br>more individual effect = stronger impact | 1 → 4<br>less → more | **2** |
| **IMPACT INDEX** (I_AI)<br>sum of impact factors | 1 → 24<br>low → high | **16** |
| **FORESIGHT FACTOR**<br>levels of foresight available | A → F<br>many → few<br>sources sources | **A** |
| **QUALITY**<br>net effect of Wild Card | + positive<br>- negative<br>± both | **(−)** |

159

# U.S. GOVERNMENT REDESIGNED

In the face of ubiquitous computing and communications, the growing influence of corporations, and the structural inability of present government to adapt quickly to rapidly changing situations, the U.S. government is dramatically redesigned. Everyone has the ability to interface directly with the governmental system at many different levels through the Internet. The role of elected representatives changes.

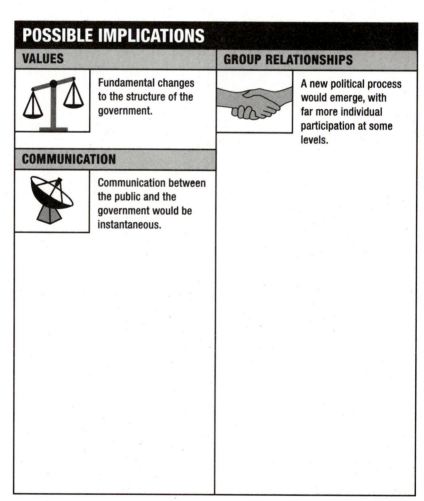

## POSSIBLE IMPLICATIONS

**VALUES**

Fundamental changes to the structure of the government.

**COMMUNICATION**

Communication between the public and the government would be instantaneous.

**GROUP RELATIONSHIPS**

A new political process would emerge, with far more individual participation at some levels.

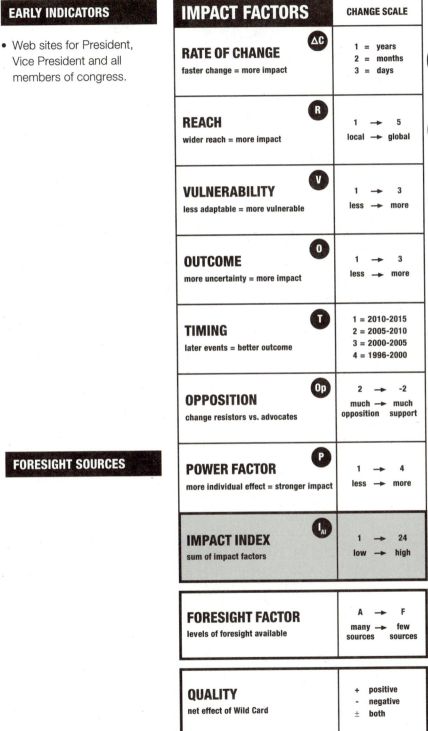

- Web sites for President, Vice President and all members of congress.

| IMPACT FACTORS | CHANGE SCALE | |
|---|---|---|
| **RATE OF CHANGE** ΔC<br>faster change = more impact | 1 = years<br>2 = months<br>3 = days | 1 |
| **REACH** R<br>wider reach = more impact | 1 → 5<br>local → global | 3 |
| **VULNERABILITY** V<br>less adaptable = more vulnerable | 1 → 3<br>less → more | 1 |
| **OUTCOME** O<br>more uncertainty = more impact | 1 → 3<br>less → more | 1 |
| **TIMING** T<br>later events = better outcome | 1 = 2010-2015<br>2 = 2005-2010<br>3 = 2000-2005<br>4 = 1996-2000 | 3 |
| **OPPOSITION** Op<br>change resistors vs. advocates | 2 → -2<br>much → much<br>opposition support | 2 |
| **POWER FACTOR** P<br>more individual effect = stronger impact | 1 → 4<br>less → more | 1 |
| **IMPACT INDEX** I$_{AI}$<br>sum of impact factors | 1 → 24<br>low → high | 12 |
| **FORESIGHT FACTOR**<br>levels of foresight available | A → F<br>many → few<br>sources sources | A |
| **QUALITY**<br>net effect of Wild Card | + positive<br>- negative<br>± both | + |

# ELECTRONIC CASH ENABLES TAX REVOLT IN THE U.S.

Encryption becomes prevalent as commerce increasingly moves to the net. "E-Cash" is a standard currency, making it rather easy to hide the existence and source of the money. The government can no longer track the flow of funds and lose their ability to tax effectively.

## POSSIBLE IMPLICATIONS

| ACTIVITY | GROUP RELATIONSHIPS |
|---|---|
| Explosion in E-Cash firms. | Major overhaul of the U.S. government: citizens finally have lever with which to directly influence government—they can withhold money; the government scrambles to redesign the taxing process, they decrease in size and become further polarized from the rest of society. |

# WILD CARD EQUATION

## EARLY INDICATORS

- Sophisticated encryption processes.
- Rapid movement of commerce toward the Net.

## FORESIGHT SOURCES

- *Wired Magazine*
- *Computer industry press*

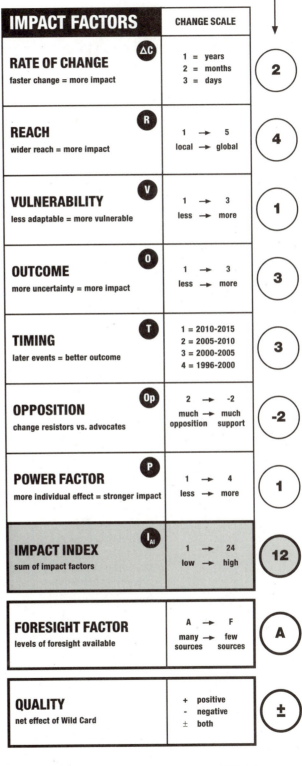

| IMPACT FACTORS | CHANGE SCALE | |
|---|---|---|
| **RATE OF CHANGE** $\Delta c$<br>faster change = more impact | 1 = years<br>2 = months<br>3 = days | **2** |
| **REACH** $R$<br>wider reach = more impact | 1 → 5<br>local → global | **4** |
| **VULNERABILITY** $V$<br>less adaptable = more vulnerable | 1 → 3<br>less → more | **1** |
| **OUTCOME** $O$<br>more uncertainty = more impact | 1 → 3<br>less → more | **3** |
| **TIMING** $T$<br>later events = better outcome | 1 = 2010-2015<br>2 = 2005-2010<br>3 = 2000-2005<br>4 = 1996-2000 | **3** |
| **OPPOSITION** $Op$<br>change resistors vs. advocates | 2 → -2<br>much → much<br>opposition support | **-2** |
| **POWER FACTOR** $P$<br>more individual effect = stronger impact | 1 → 4<br>less → more | **1** |
| **IMPACT INDEX** $I_{AI}$<br>sum of impact factors | 1 → 24<br>low → high | **12** |
| **FORESIGHT FACTOR**<br>levels of foresight available | A → F<br>many → few<br>sources sources | **A** |
| **QUALITY**<br>net effect of Wild Card | + positive<br>- negative<br>± both | **±** |

# COLLAPSE OF THE SPERM COUNT

The global sperm count collapses and significantly affects global demographics. Worldwide birth rates decrease, reducing strain on food and other resources in countries overburdened by population.

## POSSIBLE IMPLICATIONS

### VALUES

Heightened concern about other possible implications of industrial-age processes.

### PERSONAL RELATIONSHIPS

Women who want children question the virility of their mates.

### HABITAT

The environmental factors underlying the drop in sperm count— exposure to industrial toxins, for example— cause heightened concern about the implications of the industrial age processes; new environmental regulations are imposed; lower birth rates self-correct some of the global over population problem.

# WILD CARD EQUATION

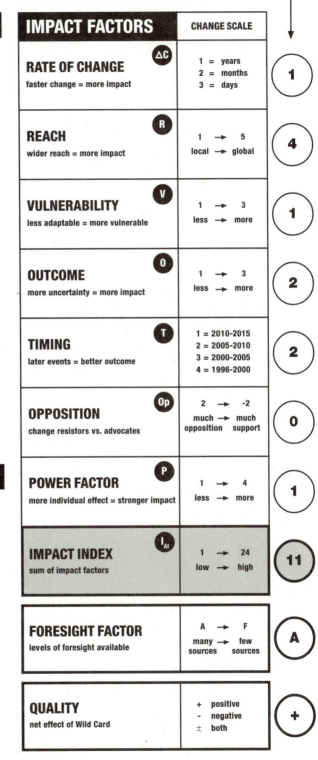

## EARLY INDICATORS

- Reduced fertility apparently related to falling sperm count seen in many areas of the world (1996).

## FORESIGHT SOURCES

- *Science News*

| IMPACT FACTORS | CHANGE SCALE | |
|---|---|---|
| **RATE OF CHANGE** $\Delta c$ <br> faster change = more impact | 1 = years <br> 2 = months <br> 3 = days | **1** |
| **REACH** R <br> wider reach = more impact | 1 → 5 <br> local → global | **4** |
| **VULNERABILITY** V <br> less adaptable = more vulnerable | 1 → 3 <br> less → more | **1** |
| **OUTCOME** O <br> more uncertainty = more impact | 1 → 3 <br> less → more | **2** |
| **TIMING** T <br> later events = better outcome | 1 = 2010-2015 <br> 2 = 2005-2010 <br> 3 = 2000-2005 <br> 4 = 1996-2000 | **2** |
| **OPPOSITION** Op <br> change resistors vs. advocates | 2 → -2 <br> much → much <br> opposition support | **0** |
| **POWER FACTOR** P <br> more individual effect = stronger impact | 1 → 4 <br> less → more | **1** |
| **IMPACT INDEX** $I_{AI}$ <br> sum of impact factors | 1 → 24 <br> low → high | **11** |
| **FORESIGHT FACTOR** <br> levels of foresight available | A → F <br> many → few <br> sources sources | **A** |
| **QUALITY** <br> net effect of Wild Card | + positive <br> - negative <br> ± both | **+** |

**165**

# RELIGIOUS RIGHT POLITICAL PARTY GAINS POWER

The religious right forms a new political party, after the Republicans are judged to be too liberal after the 1996 presidential election. In 2000, this new party wins a sweeping victory, gaining control of the United States on both national and state levels. Broad changes in legislation follow . . .

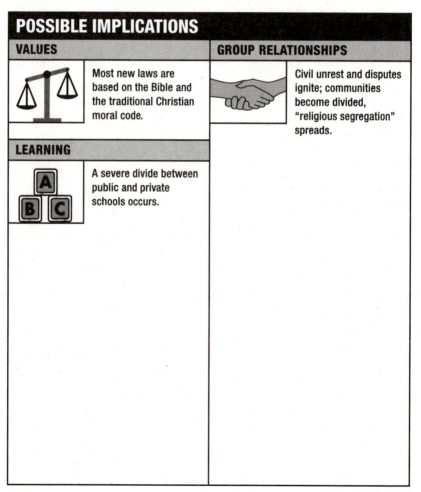

## POSSIBLE IMPLICATIONS

### VALUES

Most new laws are based on the Bible and the traditional Christian moral code.

### LEARNING

A severe divide between public and private schools occurs.

### GROUP RELATIONSHIPS

Civil unrest and disputes ignite; communities become divided, "religious segregation" spreads.

## WILD CARD EQUATION

### EARLY INDICATORS

- Pat Buchanan and Oliver North.
- Christian Television Network.
- Growth in conservative religion.
- Dramatic change in foreign relations and U.S. world involvement.
- Radical shift in government policy in areas of welfare, abortion, education.

### FORESIGHT SOURCES

- *Christianity Today Magazine*
- *Christian Booksellers Association*
- *Christian family movement*

| IMPACT FACTORS | CHANGE SCALE | |
|---|---|---|
| **RATE OF CHANGE** ΔC<br>faster change = more impact | 1 = years<br>2 = months<br>3 = days | 1 |
| **REACH** R<br>wider reach = more impact | 1 → 5<br>local → global | 1 |
| **VULNERABILITY** V<br>less adaptable = more vulnerable | 1 → 3<br>less → more | 2 |
| **OUTCOME** O<br>more uncertainty = more impact | 1 → 3<br>less → more | 2 |
| **TIMING** T<br>later events = better outcome | 1 = 2010-2015<br>2 = 2005-2010<br>3 = 2000-2005<br>4 = 1996-2000 | 3 |
| **OPPOSITION** Op<br>change resistors vs. advocates | 2 → -2<br>much → much<br>opposition support | 2 |
| **POWER FACTOR** P<br>more individual effect = stronger impact | 1 → 4<br>less → more | 3 |
| **IMPACT INDEX** $I_{AI}$<br>sum of impact factors | 1 → 24<br>low → high | 14 |
| **FORESIGHT FACTOR**<br>levels of foresight available | A → F<br>many → few<br>sources sources | A |
| **QUALITY**<br>net effect of Wild Card | + positive<br>- negative<br>± both | ± |

# ISRAEL DEFEATED IN WAR

In a surprise move, Israeli enemies neutralize the Israel Defense Force and capture the country.

## POSSIBLE IMPLICATIONS

### GROUP RELATIONSHIPS

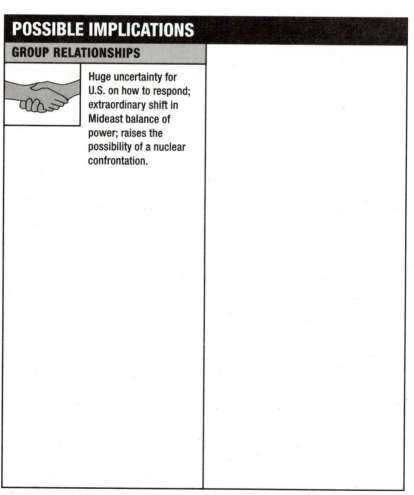

Huge uncertainty for U.S. on how to respond; extraordinary shift in Mideast balance of power; raises the possibility of a nuclear confrontation.

**EARLY INDICATORS**

| IMPACT FACTORS | CHANGE SCALE | |
|---|---|---|
| **RATE OF CHANGE** $\Delta c$<br>faster change = more impact | 1 = years<br>2 = months<br>3 = days | 1 |
| **REACH** R<br>wider reach = more impact | 1 → 5<br>local → global | 4 |
| **VULNERABILITY** V<br>less adaptable = more vulnerable | 1 → 3<br>less → more | 2 |
| **OUTCOME** O<br>more uncertainty = more impact | 1 → 3<br>less → more | 3 |
| **TIMING** T<br>later events = better outcome | 1 = 2010-2015<br>2 = 2005-2010<br>3 = 2000-2005<br>4 = 1996-2000 | 4 |
| **OPPOSITION** Op<br>change resistors vs. advocates | 2 → -2<br>much → much<br>opposition support | 2 |
| **POWER FACTOR** P<br>more individual effect = stronger impact | 1 → 4<br>less → more | 1 |
| **IMPACT INDEX** $I_{AI}$<br>sum of impact factors | 1 → 24<br>low → high | 17 |
| **FORESIGHT FACTOR**<br>levels of foresight available | A → F<br>many → few<br>sources sources | C |
| **QUALITY**<br>net effect of Wild Card | + positive<br>- negative<br>± both | - |

**FORESIGHT SOURCES**

# INFORMATION WAR BREAKS OUT

What starts as a minor tactic in a trade conflict between two major countries, expands into a full-blown information war with monetary and financial systems — as well as the media — being targeted.

## POSSIBLE IMPLICATIONS

### VALUES

Infowar would threaten the underpinnings of whole social systems in advanced countries.

### ACTIVITY

Business would rally to find alternative communication methods; widespread panic.

### COMMUNICATION

Potential vulnerability of Internet and other critical information systems.

### GROUP RELATIONSHIPS

The battle could spill over to involve most major countries.

## WILD CARD EQUATION

- Many countries now working on infowar methods.

- *InfoWarCon Convention*
- *National Computer Security Association*

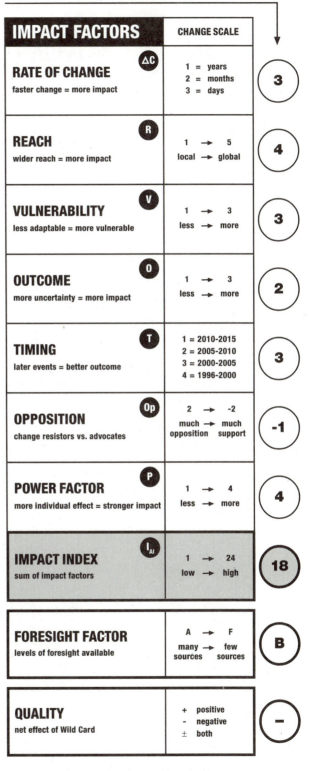

| IMPACT FACTORS | CHANGE SCALE | |
|---|---|---|
| **RATE OF CHANGE** (ΔC) <br> faster change = more impact | 1 = years <br> 2 = months <br> 3 = days | 3 |
| **REACH** (R) <br> wider reach = more impact | 1 → 5 <br> local → global | 4 |
| **VULNERABILITY** (V) <br> less adaptable = more vulnerable | 1 → 3 <br> less → more | 3 |
| **OUTCOME** (O) <br> more uncertainty = more impact | 1 → 3 <br> less → more | 2 |
| **TIMING** (T) <br> later events = better outcome | 1 = 2010-2015 <br> 2 = 2005-2010 <br> 3 = 2000-2005 <br> 4 = 1996-2000 | 3 |
| **OPPOSITION** (Op) <br> change resistors vs. advocates | 2 → -2 <br> much → much <br> opposition support | -1 |
| **POWER FACTOR** (P) <br> more individual effect = stronger impact | 1 → 4 <br> less → more | 4 |
| **IMPACT INDEX** (I$_{AI}$) <br> sum of impact factors | 1 → 24 <br> low → high | 18 |
| **FORESIGHT FACTOR** <br> levels of foresight available | A → F <br> many → few <br> sources sources | B |
| **QUALITY** <br> net effect of Wild Card | + positive <br> - negative <br> ± both | – |

# CIVIL WAR BETWEEN SOVIET STATES GOES NUCLEAR

A border war between states of the former Soviet Union escalates into a nuclear exchange.

## POSSIBLE IMPLICATIONS

### GROUP RELATIONSHIPS

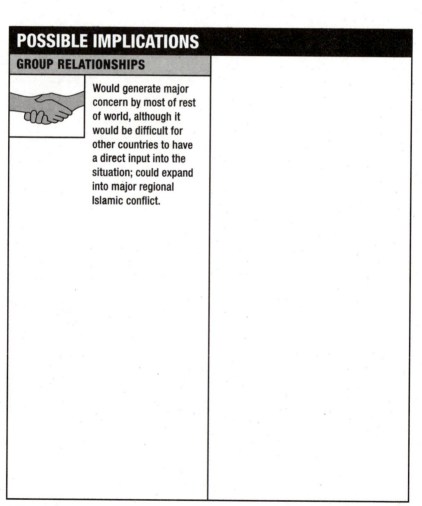

Would generate major concern by most of rest of world, although it would be difficult for other countries to have a direct input into the situation; could expand into major regional Islamic conflict.

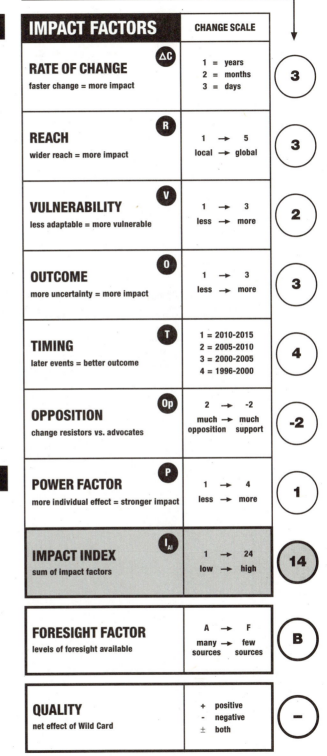

- Unhappiness between former Soviet Union states.
- Continued possession of nuclear weapons by former Soviet Union states.

### FORESIGHT SOURCES

| IMPACT FACTORS | CHANGE SCALE | |
|---|---|---|
| **RATE OF CHANGE** ΔC<br>faster change = more impact | 1 = years<br>2 = months<br>3 = days | **3** |
| **REACH** R<br>wider reach = more impact | 1 → 5<br>local → global | **3** |
| **VULNERABILITY** V<br>less adaptable = more vulnerable | 1 → 3<br>less → more | **2** |
| **OUTCOME** O<br>more uncertainty = more impact | 1 → 3<br>less → more | **3** |
| **TIMING** T<br>later events = better outcome | 1 = 2010-2015<br>2 = 2005-2010<br>3 = 2000-2005<br>4 = 1996-2000 | **4** |
| **OPPOSITION** Op<br>change resistors vs. advocates | 2 → -2<br>much → much<br>opposition support | **-2** |
| **POWER FACTOR** P<br>more individual effect = stronger impact | 1 → 4<br>less → more | **1** |
| **IMPACT INDEX** I$_{AI}$<br>sum of impact factors | 1 → 24<br>low → high | **14** |
| **FORESIGHT FACTOR**<br>levels of foresight available | A → F<br>many → few<br>sources sources | **B** |
| **QUALITY**<br>net effect of Wild Card | + positive<br>- negative<br>± both | **—** |

# MASS MIGRATIONS

A significant part of the country, or the world, becomes an entirely unde-sirable place to live. Due to a combination of any number of factors — such as a natural disaster or environmental crisis; or a technological break-through that makes local skills obsolete — a large population of residents are forced to migrate. The adjacent areas are unable to cope with the load of incomers.

## POSSIBLE IMPLICATIONS

### HABITAT

 Mass arrival of new people would strain local social, educational and transportation systems.

### ACTIVITY

Émigrés would require jobs in their new location.

### GROUP RELATIONSHIPS

 Conflicts would ignite between émigrés and residents of areas to which they move; military would be called out to deal with the situations uncontrol-lable by local law enforcement.

# WILD CARD EQUATION

## EARLY INDICATORS

- Increasing number of people whose skills are associated with old technologies.
- Increase in disasters, like Chernobyl.
- Likely increase in anomalous events which would produce émigrés.

## FORESIGHT SOURCES

| IMPACT FACTORS | CHANGE SCALE | |
|---|---|---|
| **RATE OF CHANGE** $\Delta c$<br>faster change = more impact | 1 = years<br>2 = months<br>3 = days | **2** |
| **REACH** R<br>wider reach = more impact | 1 → 5<br>local → global | **3** |
| **VULNERABILITY** V<br>less adaptable = more vulnerable | 1 → 3<br>less → more | **3** |
| **OUTCOME** O<br>more uncertainty = more impact | 1 → 3<br>less → more | **2** |
| **TIMING** T<br>later events = better outcome | 1 = 2010-2015<br>2 = 2005-2010<br>3 = 2000-2005<br>4 = 1996-2000 | **3** |
| **OPPOSITION** Op<br>change resistors vs. advocates | 2 → -2<br>much → much<br>opposition support | **-2** |
| **POWER FACTOR** P<br>more individual effect = stronger impact | 1 → 4<br>less → more | **2** |
| **IMPACT INDEX** $I_{AI}$<br>sum of impact factors | 1 → 24<br>low → high | **13** |
| **FORESIGHT FACTOR**<br>levels of foresight available | A → F<br>many → few<br>sources sources | **A** |
| **QUALITY**<br>net effect of Wild Card | + positive<br>- negative<br>± both | **–** |

# WESTERN STATE SECEDES FROM THE U.S.

Finally fed up with federal government requirements, Hawaiian, or Pacific Northwest movements for secession rapidly build up steam and result in a popular vote for leaving the United States.

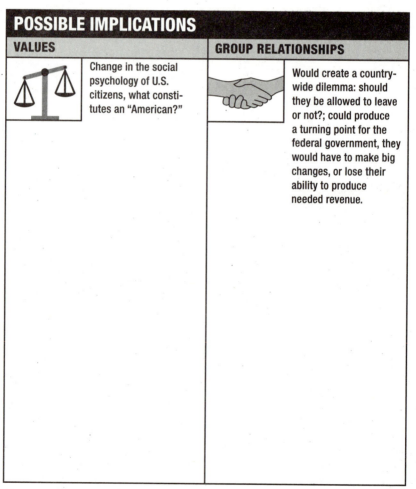

## POSSIBLE IMPLICATIONS

### VALUES

Change in the social psychology of U.S. citizens, what constitutes an "American?"

### GROUP RELATIONSHIPS

Would create a country-wide dilemma: should they be allowed to leave or not?; could produce a turning point for the federal government, they would have to make big changes, or lose their ability to produce needed revenue.

- Existing secession movements in Hawaii and Pacific Northwest…"with no discernible enemies or threats, why should we pay into a big defense bill?"

- Freeman/militia movements.

- Unfunded mandates by federal government to states.

### FORESIGHT SOURCES

| IMPACT FACTORS | CHANGE SCALE | |
|---|---|---|
| **RATE OF CHANGE** $\Delta$C<br>faster change = more impact | 1 = years<br>2 = months<br>3 = days | 1 |
| **REACH** R<br>wider reach = more impact | 1 → 5<br>local → global | 2 |
| **VULNERABILITY** V<br>less adaptable = more vulnerable | 1 → 3<br>less → more | 1 |
| **OUTCOME** O<br>more uncertainty = more impact | 1 → 3<br>less → more | 3 |
| **TIMING** T<br>later events = better outcome | 1 = 2010-2015<br>2 = 2005-2010<br>3 = 2000-2005<br>4 = 1996-2000 | 2 |
| **OPPOSITION** Op<br>change resistors vs. advocates | 2 → -2<br>much → much<br>opposition support | 2 |
| **POWER FACTOR** P<br>more individual effect = stronger impact | 1 → 4<br>less → more | 1 |
| **IMPACT INDEX** I$_{AI}$<br>sum of impact factors | 1 → 24<br>low → high | 12 |
| **FORESIGHT FACTOR**<br>levels of foresight available | A → F<br>many → few<br>sources sources | B |
| **QUALITY**<br>net effect of Wild Card | + positive<br>- negative<br>± both | ± |

# COLLAPSE OF THE UNITED NATIONS

A major event or combination of events destroys the credibility of the United Nations. Major countries lose confidence and pull out en masse.

## POSSIBLE IMPLICATIONS

### GROUP RELATIONSHIPS

Rapid scramble to develop a new forum for international dialogue; opportunity to design a new, more effective organization; smaller countries use the opportunity to "gang up" against larger ones.

# WILD CARD EQUATION

## EARLY INDICATORS

- Notorious inefficiency of UN.
- Increasing role of non-governmental organizations.

## FORESIGHT SOURCES

| IMPACT FACTORS | CHANGE SCALE | |
|---|---|---|
| **RATE OF CHANGE** $\Delta c$<br>faster change = more impact | 1 = years<br>2 = months<br>3 = days | **2** |
| **REACH** $R$<br>wider reach = more impact | 1 → 5<br>local → global | **3** |
| **VULNERABILITY** $V$<br>less adaptable = more vulnerable | 1 → 3<br>less → more | **1** |
| **OUTCOME** $O$<br>more uncertainty = more impact | 1 → 3<br>less → more | **3** |
| **TIMING** $T$<br>later events = better outcome | 1 = 2010-2015<br>2 = 2005-2010<br>3 = 2000-2005<br>4 = 1996-2000 | **3** |
| **OPPOSITION** $Op$<br>change resistors vs. advocates | 2 → -2<br>much → much<br>opposition support | **-2** |
| **POWER FACTOR** $P$<br>more individual effect = stronger impact | 1 → 4<br>less → more | **1** |
| **IMPACT INDEX** $I_{AI}$<br>sum of impact factors | 1 → 24<br>low → high | **11** |
| **FORESIGHT FACTOR**<br>levels of foresight available | A → F<br>many → few<br>sources sources | **B** |
| **QUALITY**<br>net effect of Wild Card | + positive<br>- negative<br>± both | **±** |

# END OF THE NATION STATE

The role of government is relegated to local affairs, they simply cannot keep up with the increasing pace of changes in global communications. As all types of information can be transported on the Internet — without regard to national borders — large corporations become increasingly transnational, and it becomes impossible to effectively define sovereignty. Corporations, and alliances of corporations ("The Group of Seventy") become the de facto forces that determine economic, defense, and diplomatic policy as they are the only institutions that can react and adapt effectively to a quick changes in social systems and world affairs.

## POSSIBLE IMPLICATIONS

### COMMUNICATION

New methods of responding to citizen concerns and interests are developed, which would revolve around a Web or cable connection enabling the public to interface with the new "government" on many different levels, up to and including global.

### GROUP RELATIONSHIPS

Government heads become like monarchies, primarily ceremonial; the "economics-only" orientation of major corporations would transform to include a much broader repertoire of interests.

- Exploding growth of Internet/World Wide Web.
- Non-national nature of large corporations.
- Global nature of increasing problems/issues.
- Structural impediments to the acceleration of governmental response to change.

| IMPACT FACTORS | CHANGE SCALE | |
|---|---|---|
| **RATE OF CHANGE** ΔC<br>faster change = more impact | 1 = years<br>2 = months<br>3 = days | **1** |
| **REACH** R<br>wider reach = more impact | 1 → 5<br>local → global | **2** |
| **VULNERABILITY** V<br>less adaptable = more vulnerable | 1 → 3<br>less → more | **1** |
| **OUTCOME** O<br>more uncertainty = more impact | 1 → 3<br>less → more | **1** |
| **TIMING** T<br>later events = better outcome | 1 = 2010-2015<br>2 = 2005-2010<br>3 = 2000-2005<br>4 = 1996-2000 | **1** |
| **OPPOSITION** Op<br>change resistors vs. advocates | 2 → -2<br>much → much<br>opposition support | **-1** |
| **POWER FACTOR** P<br>more individual effect = stronger impact | 1 → 4<br>less → more | **1** |
| **IMPACT INDEX** $I_{AI}$<br>sum of impact factors | 1 → 24<br>low → high | **6** |
| **FORESIGHT FACTOR**<br>levels of foresight available | A → F<br>many → few<br>sources sources | **A** |
| **QUALITY**<br>net effect of Wild Card | + positive<br>- negative<br>± both | **+** |

# MEXICAN ECONOMY FAILS AND THE U.S. TAKES OVER

After the Mexican economy catastrophically fails, Mexican leadership asks the U.S. to take over the country in order to fix the situation. Even in the face of extraordinary domestic immigration implications, the U.S. agrees.

## POSSIBLE IMPLICATIONS

| COMMUNICATION | GROUP RELATIONSHIPS |
|---|---|
| New language dilemmas. | Dramatic changes in practical politics of the new nation; massive changes in national economics; increased U.S. illegal immigration problems; tremendous tension between races. |

## EARLY INDICATORS

- Poll in 1995 shows 85% of Mexicans believe that the only way that their problems can be solved is by becoming a part of the U.S.

- 600,000 businesses failed in Mexico in first 11 months of 1995.

## FORESIGHT SOURCES

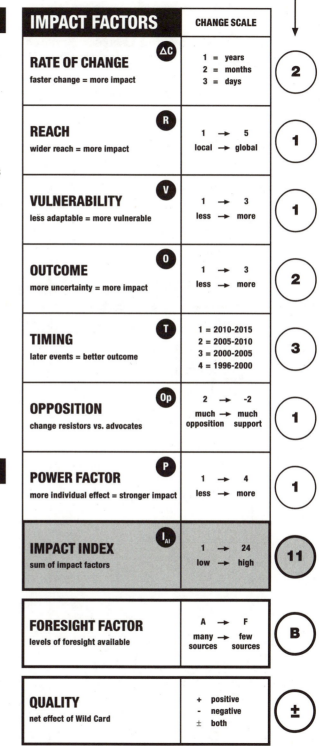

| IMPACT FACTORS | CHANGE SCALE | |
|---|---|---|
| **RATE OF CHANGE** $\Delta c$<br>faster change = more impact | 1 = years<br>2 = months<br>3 = days | 2 |
| **REACH** R<br>wider reach = more impact | 1 → 5<br>local → global | 1 |
| **VULNERABILITY** V<br>less adaptable = more vulnerable | 1 → 3<br>less → more | 1 |
| **OUTCOME** O<br>more uncertainty = more impact | 1 → 3<br>less → more | 2 |
| **TIMING** T<br>later events = better outcome | 1 = 2010-2015<br>2 = 2005-2010<br>3 = 2000-2005<br>4 = 1996-2000 | 3 |
| **OPPOSITION** Op<br>change resistors vs. advocates | 2 → -2<br>much → much<br>opposition support | 1 |
| **POWER FACTOR** P<br>more individual effect = stronger impact | 1 → 4<br>less → more | 1 |
| **IMPACT INDEX** $I_{AI}$<br>sum of impact factors | 1 → 24<br>low → high | 11 |
| **FORESIGHT FACTOR**<br>levels of foresight available | A → F<br>many → few<br>sources sources | B |
| **QUALITY**<br>net effect of Wild Card | + positive<br>- negative<br>± both | ± |

# SOCIETY TURNS AWAY FROM THE MILITARY

American society evolves values that are at odds with traditional principles held by the military. The time arrives when Americans take the effectual stand that, "The military no longer represents who we are." The result is a rapid decrease in funding for the Department of Defense, and the military is relegated to mercenary-like roles outside of the country.

## POSSIBLE IMPLICATIONS

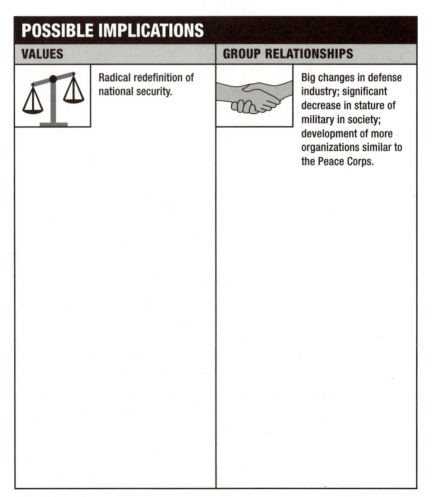

| VALUES | GROUP RELATIONSHIPS |
|---|---|
| Radical redefinition of national security. | Big changes in defense industry; significant decrease in stature of military in society; development of more organizations similar to the Peace Corps. |

# WILD CARD EQUATION

## EARLY INDICATORS

- Marines indicate contempt for the direction that majority public values are heading (1995).
- 85% of business school graduates admitted to cheating (1996).
- U.S. business loses $2 billion per week to employee and other theft.

## FORESIGHT SOURCES

- *University and non-profit ethics programs.*

| IMPACT FACTORS | CHANGE SCALE | |
|---|---|---|
| **RATE OF CHANGE** $\Delta C$ <br> faster change = more impact | 1 = years <br> 2 = months <br> 3 = days | **1** |
| **REACH** R <br> wider reach = more impact | 1 → 5 <br> local → global | **1** |
| **VULNERABILITY** V <br> less adaptable = more vulnerable | 1 → 3 <br> less → more | **1** |
| **OUTCOME** O <br> more uncertainty = more impact | 1 → 3 <br> less → more | **1** |
| **TIMING** T <br> later events = better outcome | 1 = 2010-2015 <br> 2 = 2005-2010 <br> 3 = 2000-2005 <br> 4 = 1996-2000 | **2** |
| **OPPOSITION** Op <br> change resistors vs. advocates | 2 → -2 <br> much → much <br> opposition support | **-1** |
| **POWER FACTOR** P <br> more individual effect = stronger impact | 1 → 4 <br> less → more | **1** |
| **IMPACT INDEX** $I_{AI}$ <br> sum of impact factors | 1 → 24 <br> low → high | **6** |
| **FORESIGHT FACTOR** <br> levels of foresight available | A → F <br> many → few <br> sources sources | **A** |
| **QUALITY** <br> net effect of Wild Card | + positive <br> - negative <br> ± both | **±** |

# SELECTED RESOURCES

## Consciousness/Brain Research

Institute for Noetic Sciences
475 Gate Five Road, Suite 3
Sausalito CA 94965

Fetzer Institute
9292 W. Kalamazoo Ave.
Kalamazoo MI 49009

Brain/Mind Bulletin
PO Box 42211
Los Angeles CA 90042

## Extraordinary Technology

MCC Corporation
3500 West Balcones Center Dr.
Austin TX 78759

MIT Media Lab
Neisner Building
Massachusetts Institute of Technology
Cambridge, MA 02139

Sarnoff Research Center Inc
201 Washington Rd.
Princeton, NJ 08540-6449

(Philosophy of Technology)
William VanDusen Wishard
World-Trends Research
1805 Wainwright Drive
Reson, VA 22090

BT Laboratories
B55 G28 Martlesham Heath
Ipswich, Suffolk England IP5 7RE

## Energy

Institute for Advanced Research at Austin
4030 Braker Lane West, Suite 300
Austin, TX 78759

Rocky Mountain Institute
1739 Snowmass Creek Road
Snowmass, CO 81654-3851

Clean Energy Technology, Inc.
2074 20th St.
Sarasota, FL 34234

# SELECTED RESOURCES

**Social Values & Futurism**

Society for Scientific Exploration
Prof. Laurence W. Fredrick
Dept. of Astronomy,
Univ. of Virginia, Box 3818
CharlottesvilleVA 22903-0818

The World Future Society
7910 Woodmont Ave., Suite 450
Bethesda MD 20814
1-800-989-8274

Global Business Network
5900-X Hollis Street, P.O. Box 8395
Emeryville, CA, 94608

Copenhagen Institute for Future Studies
Pilestraede 59
Copenhagen K, Denmark DK-1112

The Institute for the Future
2744 Sand Hill Road
Menlo Park, CA 94025-7097

# BOOK ORDER FORM

***Out of the Blue: Wild Cards and Other Big Future Surprises - $13.⁹⁵***

*Out of The Blue* is a rapid ride through almost 80 future scenarios that will get you "out of the box," teach you to anticipate and plan for big change, and effectively manage the surprises along the way.

**Also by John Petersen . . .**

***The Road to 2015: Profiles of the Future - $18.⁹⁵***

*#1 Bestseller on World Future Society List*

"*The Road to 2015* is the best book currently in print on changing trends, enabling technologies, and other emerging factors that are shaping the future of society." **Oliver Markley, Professor, Graduate Program in Studies of the Future, University of Houston, Clear Lake**

---

Name _____

Address _____

City/State/Zip _____

Telephone _____ Fax _____

Email _____

| **Discount Schedule** |
|:---:|
| **2-4 books = 20% • 5-20 books = 25%** |
| **21-49 books = 30% • 50+ books = 40%** |

*Out of the Blue*      Quantity _____ x $13.⁹⁵  = $ _____

*The Road to 2015*   Quantity _____ x $18.⁹⁵  = $ _____

Discount               % _____              − $ _____

VA residents add 4.5% sales tax              = $ _____

Shipping [$3 ship/handle + $1 each additional book]   + $ _____
Call for international and overnight rates.

**Total Due   $ _____**

**Ship to (if different than above):**

Name _____

Address _____

City/State/Zip _____

---

Please mail this sheet with check or money order and make payable to:

**The Arlington Institute**
**2101 Crystal Plaza Arcade #136, Arlington, VA, 22202**
**703.243.7070 • fax 703.243.7086**
**johnp@arlinst.org • www.arlinst.org**

*Thank you for your order!*